You Sheriff of Me Town

Where You Have All the Power

Dr. Julia Bain, LPCC, NCC, CEAP

Copyright © 2021 by Julia Bain

All rights reserved. In accordance with the U.S. Copyright Act of 1976, the scanning, uploading, and electronic sharing of any part of this book without the permission of the publisher constitute unlawful piracy and theft of the author's intellectual property. If you would like to use material from the book (other than for review purposes), prior written permission must be obtained by contacting the publisher at admin@iamsherriewalton.com. Reviewers may quote brief passages in reviews.

Walton Publishing House
Houston, Texas
www.waltonpublishinghouse.com

Printed in the United States of America

The advice found within may not be suitable for every individual. This work is purchased with the understanding that neither the author nor the publisher, are held responsible for any results. Neither author nor publisher assumes responsibility for errors, omissions, or contrary interpretations of the subject matter herein. Any perceived disparagement of an individual or organization is a misinterpretation. This book is not intended as a substitute for the medical advice of physicians. The reader should regularly consult a physician in matters relating to his/her health and particularly with respect to any symptoms that may require diagnosis or medical attention.

Some names and identifying details have been changed to protect the privacy of individuals.

Definitions found within this book are from the Oxford American Writer's Thesaurus, Second Edition, Compiled by Christine A. Lindberg, 2008, as well as Webster's New World College Dictionary Fifth Edition, 2014.

Library of Congress Cataloging-in-Publication Data under -
ISBN: 978-1-953993-06-9 herein.

Author photograph by Kim Jew Photography

Contents

Introduction	11
CHAPTER 1 You Are the Sheriff of Me Town	17
CHAPTER 2 What Are the Laws in Me Town?	30
CHAPTER 3 What do You Value as Sheriff?	40
CHAPTER 4 Own Your Decisions, Sheriff	53
CHAPTER 5 Your Words Are Your Path, Sheriff	62
CHAPTER 6 Run Me Town With Positive Perspective	74
CHAPTER 7 All of Your Choices Are in the Palm of Your Hand	80
CHAPTER 8 The Power Badge	102
CHAPTER 9 Measuring Your Mental Strength	113
CHAPTER 10 Measuring Your Physical Strength	126

CHAPTER 11
Measuring Your Spiritual Strength			138

CHAPTER 12
Measuring Your Social Strength			145

CHAPTER 13
Measuring Your Sexual Strength			153

CHAPTER 14
Measuring Your Emotional Strength			159

Resource: The Me Town Sheriff's A-Z Guide		174
Final Thoughts					190
Epilogue						191
Acknowledgments					192
About The Author					193

Dedication

*This book is dedicated to Kimberly Sherah Riebsomer.
It is because of her inspiration, love, and encouragement that
this book unfolded into everything it was intended to be.*

"When I first took office and met Dr. Julia Bain, I asked her to share what her job was like as EAP Manager for the City of Albuquerque. Without hesitation, she responded, 'I help City employees use their own courage to make good decisions.' That conversation has always stuck with me. Dr. Bain continues her mission through this book, and many more people will have the opportunity to grow stronger and feel empowered because of it."

Mayor Timothy M. Keller, Albuquerque, New Mexico

"Me Town is a refreshing throwback to the old west where handshakes were honored and folks didn't dare shirk duties out on the range. Me Town is a fun hayride of personal accomplishment, professional expertise and a creative re-design of the clinical space."

Andrew Garrison
Award-winning author of Wellness In Mind and Being Image with co-author Dr. Sally Severino.

"Dr. Julia Bain has brought her strident and caring spirit to this book. It is a generous sharing of her own experience, both professional and personal, reflected in this unique roadmap to living our lives consciously stronger, and inevitably happier! Kudos!"

Lynnette Geschwind
Director of Equity, Diversity, and ADA Accessibility
State of Minnesota DOT

"In the opening paragraphs of You Are the Sheriff of Me Town, Dr. Julia Bain lays down some important advice that every human being should know: That you are responsible for your own happiness. With practical steps for how to achieve this end, many, many people's lives could be turned around by taking her straight-shooting advice to heart."

James E. Porter,
CEO, StressStop
Author: Stop Stress this Minute

"In a world in which blame is rampant and personal accountability is in short supply comes Dr. Julia Bain with the powerful truth that self-determination and individual decisions are what matters, not pointing fingers, and surely not in wasting our time focusing on the things we usually can't control, like our circumstances, and personal and work environments. Dr. Bain uses positive insights into how WE, as individuals, and no one else, possess the power of change. The analogy to the Old West kept it a lively read the whole way through!"

Mike Jacquart
Editor of Journal of Employee Assistance (for EAPA) and author of A Century of Excellence: 100 Greatest Packers Of All Time, available on Amazon.

"I've known Dr. Julia Bain for nearly 30 years, and have benefited greatly over the years from her lively, thoughtful, and positive approach to life and how to live it. This excellent book is a saddle bag full of tools to empower a satisfying life, with important lessons for overcoming tough situations and bad hombres. Julia's experience as a counselor is a helpful rope coiled through the text. If you're looking for a thoughtful, meaningful, and lively text written by someone who's ridden these dusty trails, saddle up and enjoy the read!"

David S. Campbell, MPA, JD
Retired Attorney, U.S. Diplomat, and City Manager
Albuquerque, NM

"For anyone wishing to feel empowered in their life, I highly recommend this book. You'll be glad you partook in the journey through "Me Town," as it is a way of life you'll continue long after completing the book. Having known Dr. Julia Bain for over two decades it is a pleasure to see her passion for empowering others in book form. I found the information helpful, well organized, easy to put into practice and most of all engaging. In summary, the journey this book takes you on is a life changing experience you owe yourself and those you care about at the beginning and the end."

Rick Vinnay, LCSW, CEAP
Executive Director of The Solutions Group,
Wellness & EAP Programs

Message to My Readers

This handbook is a groundbreaking guide to help you understand that you have all the power necessary to effectively run your life. It will introduce you to the joys and benefits of living in 'Me Town' and provide you with the tools you need to confidently navigate your choices, fears, beliefs and values. You will soon understand chances and circumstances beyond your control will both test and help you evaluate if there needs to be any new beliefs generated, not from your emotions but rather from helpful evidence that you have discovered along life's trail. These new beliefs will give you renewed self-assurance and strengthen the decisions you make in your life, now known as 'Me Town.'

Did you know that you can create the world you want to live in by taking charge as the Sheriff, rather than feeling helpless, fearful, alone or unworthy? As you turn the pages, you will learn to steer your horse (be sure to give him or her a name) by turning your head towards the direction you want to move in, knowing it is you giving the commands of where you want to go. Self-doubt will be left in the dust behind you, kicked up by the horse you ride on. Keep your chin up and look towards the route of where you want to ride, and your horse will take you there. Let yourself grow into and change gently, for if you move too quickly you may lose your balance.

As you ride through Me Town, maintain a stable position with the rest of your body, giving a slight twist of your hips when you want to veer slightly and go forward to your way of choice. Make sure you do not rotate too abruptly and you will not lose your balance. Just have the knowledge you are learning how to ride by squeezing your old beliefs gently out of the picture and making the changes you are attempting to complete. Encourage your horse to be cooperative so you may rotate yourself in your desired direction. As you increase your speed, remember to trust your horse's rhythm and know you are strong enough to hold on, you are not going to fall off.

Changing your mind will take some practice, so be patient and stick with it. A confident grasp of encouraging self-talk will let your horse know you wish to go forward. It is time to travel on a new journey and become unstoppable!

Introduction

How did a scrappy little girl from St. Louis, Missouri, growing up in Affton, a suburb located in south St. Louis county, end up writing this book for you? It is simple – I want to help you to become stronger and know with every cell of your body and soul that no one is in charge of you, except you. I considered titling this book, "Becoming Stronger," but I did not want you to think this was a workout book for your body. I also considered titling the book, "You Are What You Think," but you as an individual are so much more complex than that. The mindfulness movement is trending right now and I did not want you to decide this was just about getting your mind right, so others cannot ensnare and tangle you in their drama with manipulation, although that concept is addressed within these pages. "You are the Sheriff of Me Town" was more fitting because it embodied my love for westerns and combined my life's story of fighting for the voiceless and equipping them with the tools needed to find their voice and stand in their power.

When I was growing up, I was drawn to watching old westerns on television from as early as I can remember, especially if Doris Day was starring in it, and I used to set up old western themed play areas in the front yard of my home. My bike was my horse and my toys were my weapons. A family friend noticed I was always dressed up as a cowgirl with boots, a hat, and a scarf so she gifted me my first toy rifle for my birthday. That was a gamechanger, and if a psychic or an astrologer or any of those people who are really good at seeing the future had told me someday, I would grow up and live in the great state of New Mexico and help others become their own Sheriff, I would have responded, "What am I going to have to do to make *that* happen?" I believe they would have replied, "More adventures than you can ever imagine."

Even then I knew I was a survivor from the many horrific people who surrounded children and abused them, believing they could get away with it. I always fought back. Maybe because I was fortunate enough to have an amazing father who showed me what unconditional love was and taught me from the beginning of my life that my worth did not have to be proven to anyone, it simply existed because I was born. He instilled that in me not only with his words but by his behavior. My dad always treated me with respect and admired me by pointing out the details of my personality and celebrating them as belonging to me. In turn, I grew up with a great passion for wanting to give this gift to others because it became my deepest strength –my identity that no one could ever take away from me. As I grew older, I wanted to pay it forward.

You Are the Sheriff of Me Town evolved from a life comprised of adventure and disaster, love and hate, trust and betrayal, hunger and thirst, disappointment and rage, uproarious laughter and deeply emotional, mental, spiritual pain and torment...just like I am sure you have experienced before.

INTRODUCTION

My uniqueness was realized when I was just a little girl who played with toy guns, trucks, and army men, hauling my dolls high up into the branches of the tree in my front yard, working as sentries helping me protect the property. I would position my toy guns in front of the dolls and together, we would all wait for trouble to come along so we could take charge and protect the innocent; the people who did not believe they had a voice or a good enough swing for an effective punch. Back in the 60s and 70s, this type of girl was called a "Tomboy" although I never thought of myself that way.

I have always fought for the underdog. Maybe you know what it felt like to be that girl in the bathroom surrounded by bullies ready to pounce on you because you looked different, or because you were a sensitive kid and an "easy target," or simply because you were outnumbered and frozen with fear. Well, I was the girl who walked into that restroom to protect you as I yelled, 'Everybody get out or somebody in here is going to get hurt and it's not going to be her!' and then they quickly exited. Maybe you were that boy on the bus that the other boys teased and called, 'Tiny little prick!' Well, I sat down next to you and glared at them and said, 'You are about to lose a piece of you that you still want. Shut up and back down!' and they did. I was there for you then and I still am here for you now.

Of course, we are not kids any longer, but the bullies are still out there and there are many productive ways to fight back. As you read this book, we are going to explore and generate those strategies to help you enjoy your life despite what may be happening around you. This book is meant to help you become fully equipped with the confidence you need to be ready for this challenge we call life. Life does not ask your permission to place a predator in your midst, nor does it say please let me see how much grit and strength you have when it extinguishes the life of someone you adore. It will not say "thank you" when you do the right thing and make mature decisions while no one is watching. Nobody may ever know the sacrifices you have made to make the world a better place, and that is okay. We are going to get stronger, together Sheriff. You are never alone.

The most important lesson you need to remember is, no one can ever take **you** away from **you**, Sheriff. You have all the power. I want you to know you are not only free, but strong enough to make yourself into the person you have always wanted to become – one moment at a time, through trial and error, one breath at a time. You also have a basic human right that will upstage whatever life may throw your way. It pulses through your veins with every beat of your heart. It is your secret weapon. You have at the heart of your spirit the "dignity of risk." This term applies to you and everyone else on Earth. It means you have the right to self-determination, to develop your own will-power and resolve to figure out your own solutions to your challenges and problems. It is the freedom to make your own choices and decisions that build your self-esteem, developing your faith in yourself and growing your self-confidence throughout life. It means you will take risks, fail sometimes, learn what are the consequences of making certain choices, and have the opportunity to learn what is right and best for you. Giving yourself and others the chance to do what is best for oneself, and undertake the innumerable challenges of life, is what dignity of risk is all about. It is an essential human right. It applies to children, children living with disabilities, people with mental health and physical disabilities and the elderly. All people have the right to take reasonable risks so they may grow into someone better and stronger, feeling the freedom that comes with choice. Your personhood means you have the right to fail! When we do fail, we all need a variety of safety nets depending on our individual circumstances. Consider this book, along with the natural supports such as family, friends, school, work and community that you have in your life, one of your safety nets.

Let us begin and take this journey into Me Town together. This experience is all about you, I am just along for the ride. As you turn the pages and discover new ways of looking at yourself, other people and the rest of the world, know deep in your heart that these lessons, suggestions, pieces of advice, and hopefully what you will consider words of wisdom, were generated by not just what I have learned personally throughout life, but what everyone else has taught and shared with me. As the saying goes, 'When the student is ready the teacher appears.' So many people have helped and hurt me along the way, as I have been a captive audience. Ever since I can remember I have found people to be a fascinating subject, and I have been paying attention. What I have learned and want to share with you is what I hope is a memorable way to remember you are the C.E.O. of your own life:

C – Choice

E – Expert

O – Ongoing

We are all a work in progress. Put these letters behind your name and remember it is you and only you who is running this operation called "Me." Fight the temptation to believe you have lost your ability to choose. Remember you are the expert and know yourself better than anyone else. An in-charge attitude needs to be an ongoing practice. The moment you start acting like you are in charge, you will start feeling like you are.

You are the C.E.O. of Me, LLC. How does that sound?

When it feels like someone or some circumstance has stolen our life, we forget we are the head honcho and no one has the ability to do this to us. I understand that you can be caught off guard, sucker-punched by your life and your world can be shaken to the core. In reality, thinking we have control over life is our shared delusion, but we all like to believe we know what is coming next. Introducing yourself to yourself as CEO is a great way to start your path to Me Town. Make it a part of your daily self-talk to say, "I am the CEO of my life. I am CEO all of the time. I am the Sheriff of Me Town."

Now, how about we ride? Giddy up, let's go!

CHAPTER 1

You Are the Sheriff of Me Town

A wild west town, sun beating down, the wind whistling as it whips dust into a cloudy swirl that hangs in the air like dread. Tumbleweeds by the dozen blow along the ground. Several become trapped under a porch, piling up bigger and bigger as more join them with no escape. There is chaos. Over the loud banging of the piano and the laughter of "Dancin' Girls" in the saloon, you hear the loud, angry bellowing of outlaws fighting over a poker game. Looking across Main Street, two gunslingers draw their weapons and begin a shootout. Suddenly, a masked cowboy runs from the bank, firing his gun into the air as he jumps on a whinnying horse to make his getaway. And all the while the good townsfolk scream and duck for cover in terror, not wanting to look, yet unable to tear their eyes from the havoc surrounding them.

That's when you step up, firing your gun into the air. The chaos stops. Everyone freezes. The only sound is the still-whipping wind.

"Not in Me Town. Not anymore. I'm the new Sheriff, and from now on, you follow my rules."

Have you ever wanted to be in charge of everything? Actually, you already are. You manage everything that you perceive, every moment of every day. You are "The Sheriff of Me Town." You have all the power. Me Town is the place where we live inside our minds. Every choice, decision, and judgment we make belongs to who we have been, who we are now, and who we are becoming as the Sheriff of Me Town. It is important to value and think of Me Town as an actual place where you live, rather than just a whirling, busy, distracted, emotional, reactive habit mind that does its own thing. Think of Me Town as a construction project in which you build one thought, sentence, paragraph, chapter, and story at a time.

As you step into your Me Town, look around it with fresh eyes. Your personality will become a transformed character that wears a Sheriff badge over your heart and walks with the self-assurance that you now can own; you are officially in charge of you. Embrace the type of open, welcoming disposition that will change your point of view and customize who you are becoming. Do not allow for any ruts in the streets of Me Town. If you step into an old rut and it happens to throw you off balance, declare to yourself that negative self-regard and old habits of thinking and behavior are unintended holes in need of filling with fresh encouraging thoughts and supportive words. You are the brave Sheriff and you have come to your own rescue.

Have a sense of pride in Me Town because you know you are shaking it up with renewed power and energy. Give your Town a facelift every day you wake up and have another opportunity to put a shine on the Sheriff badge you wear that represents every part of you. When you take your badge off at the end of the day, you can be proud of yourself for having had the courage to build and change Me Town to your liking. Your Town, Your Way.

Depending on the day and your preferences, examples of new construction projects may include but are certainly not limited to:

Becoming More Likable to Yourself and Others: Since you spend most of your life hanging out with yourself in your own mind (Me Town), why not practice a good-natured, friendly, endearing, and loveable presentation of yourself to yourself? No matter what is going on in your life, you will feel better if you know a neighborly Sheriff is looking out for you. Positive, encouraging self-talk is a practice that merely requires paying attention to what types of conversations you are having with yourself while you are managing your town. The bonus prize is the words that now come out of your mouth to others will also be encouraging, and encouragement is a gift that can help others build their sense of hope. Hope brings with it promise, possibility, optimism and confidence. Isn't that what most people want? Go for it Sheriff, for there is nothing noble about being an angry pessimist and nay-sayer. Those are the people you don't want to hang with and that includes you.

Guarding Me Town from Self-Absorption: People who are self-absorbed are either feeling sorry for themselves ("Why is my life so hard?") or narcissistic ("I am better than other people and nobody is as good as me or has my wise beliefs or my amazing style...") you get the idea. Do not for one second develop a superiority complex and convince yourself you are worthier than another. You may be a high-quality individual or an accomplished expert, but you are not a better human being than the rest of us. Me Town is an equal opportunity place to become one's best self.

Respecting That Everyone Has Their Own Story: When you make assumptions about others, who they are, what they like and where they have been, you are practicing disrespect. You do not know anything about anyone else until they decide to tell you. There is no room for disrespect in Me Town, and some Sheriffs consider it a crime.

Knowing the Difference Between What You Want and What You Need: What you want is what you aspire to, desire, wish for, and long for. What you need is what you require, a necessity like food, water and shelter – a must have to survive. For most people needs include love. Remember this distinction to prevent confusion in Me Town. Life is confusing enough without you adding more unsureness to the pile. Be sure you know the difference, your life could depend on it.

Respecting Change as a Constant: You need to make friends with change, Sheriff. Much of your power to lead yourself and others comes from your ability and willingness to adjust, adapt, reshape, redesign, transform and evolve as a person. This requires willingness and practice. What gets in the way is that delusion we have that we can predict what is going to happen. We cannot do that. If change is our friend and we run towards it instead of away from it, we will develop the power that is often called bravery. You can find your nerve to just do it, go ahead and jump. You boldly confront what is different for you and march towards taking the risk that to be different from who you were before means you have the opportunity to be better and stronger. You will grow your courage and have the backbone of a Sheriff. One of the reasons I have always respected my clients whom I counseled is they all had this in common; the guts to make changes for themselves so they could find peace, love, and contentment, resolve issues, and move forward feeling powerful. Because they embraced changing themselves, they were reminded they could do it again and again and again. It takes a powerful Sheriff to look at yourself in the mirror and say, "I can change. I want to change. I will change."

You Are Responsible for Your Own Development: As Sheriff of Me Town, you realize that your feelings and thoughts become what you believe, so focusing on and practicing positive qualities like contentment, peace, love, joy, passion, bliss, excitement, and compassion are essential to moving you toward the life you want to live.

You control your capacity to either value and develop wisdom, or to mistakenly believe you are powerless over your life. We can either enjoy life, or we chronically suffer through our time here on Earth. Since we have free will, we can either cultivate creativity with the approximately 50,000 thoughts we have each day, or we can live on cruise control, stifled and out of touch with our creative side.

Most of us are survivors of some type of trauma. Even as we deal with the aftermath, we decide whether to reclaim our power and view ourselves as a warrior because we have survived, or to perpetually see ourselves as a victim.

The fact that you are holding this book in your hands is the result of your parents meeting each other and conceiving you at a certain moment in time. The majority of who you are is because of your DNA, the quality of your mom's pregnancy, the health and well-being of the environment you were raised in, and the choices other people made in your life. This refers to family, friends, teachers, neighbors, and other people you either never met or don't remember. In other words, most of who you are is by chance – things you did not decide for yourself.

Chance will always override our intellectual choices. However, as adults, we gain much power from practicing good decision making and approaching life's unexpected developments with thoughtfulness. Doesn't it make sense to empower yourself by practicing the one element of the universe you can control (that being your choices)? Of course it does. However, recognize that you do not have complete control over your destiny. You are but a cog in an enormous wheel called "life," and you will have to handle situations that you do not foresee. You can do it. Your decisions will help you to create your life story even as your plot twists and turns unexpectedly. Create a story of strength, Sheriff.

You are in charge of your choices and decisions. No one can take that power away from you. To help remind you who runs the town between your ears, why not call it Me Town? After all, when you think of the word "Me," what is being described is every person you have been, the individual you are now, and who you want to become. The first step is to create the Sheriff you want to be right now and forgive yourself for any unfortunate choices you have made in the past. There is a new Sheriff in town. It is you.

What kind of Sheriff are you going to be? Is your priority to make Me Town a healthy place, somewhere you want to live knowing that you have all the power?

Pulling a Manageable Weight in Your Wagon is Your Responsibility: Many wise people have said that happiness depends upon ourselves. Wise words, but how can we put this idea into practice? Allow me to paint a picture for you. Imagine everyone is pulling a wagon. In our wagons at birth is our DNA and the life circumstances we were born into. As we go through life, difficult situations, burdens and past hurts can collect in our wagon. Some wagons are very heavy, filled to the brim with worry, difficulty, troubles, and problems. The person pulling a heavy wagon appears to be burdened when they talk about their life. They do not seem to be at peace and are typically rushed and seem impatient or irritated at life. Is this you?

Almost all of us are survivors of some sort of trauma. We are warriors who have gone into battles over and over again and won. We are still here, the load in our wagons and our scars are proof of our resilience. What is in your wagon? How many past hurts are you carrying around in your mind and heart?

You can lighten your load as best you can by making wise, sensible choices. Do not pack a lot of drama and poor emotional habits that carry you away from living in and enjoying the moment. Practice not focusing on your past. When the memory enters your mind and begins to distract you, say, 'Stop Sign!' to yourself and come back to this moment. The past no longer exists except in your imagination. You do not have to pull it in your wagon any longer. You may toss it out in your pile of personal trivia where it belongs. It's over.

Practicing Financial Well-Being: Financial confidence can contribute to your peace of mind. Many people can find it challenging to practice financial well-being because there are often so many temptations that present themselves, especially when we equate our splurging as a reward for hard work. There are of course some times when this makes sense, and other times splurging may create more turmoil for you in the end. Let's look at this example; You see a beautiful red convertible sports car advertised in the newspaper, it's the make and model you have dreamed about since high school. Your first impulse is to call the number and ask when you can drive over and take a look. Then, you remember you have a new construction project going on in Me Town; you just took out a $28,000 loan about six months ago when you bought your spouse a new jeep to celebrate turning 40 years old. You know for a fact your dream convertible is going to be over $30,000, and you just started paying college tuition for your 18-year-old smarty pants daughter. What do you do Sheriff? It would be wise to think, 'There will be other convertibles that drive into my life when I have more disposable income to blow on a toy.' You can smile to yourself and look forward to buying the perfect ride to celebrate *your* next milestone birthday. You feel confident financially because you know you are not a millionaire (yet) and take a deep breath in relief because of the healthy financial choices you have made up to this moment. You have no worries about making ends meet in the next five years. If the roof starts leaking? No freaking out will be necessary because you have put your extra money in a savings account designated for; ***emergencies only.***

Work to Eliminate Confusion: One way to do this is to take time for simple daily meditation. Take a deep breath and light a candle. Look at the flame for a few minutes and ask yourself, 'What do I need?' Listen to your thoughts. When you practice this exercise daily you will notice that if not addressed, your mind will keep bringing up the same issues over and over again. Do not be judgmental, just pay attention and write down in a notebook what seems to keep popping up. Use your positive self-talk to conquer negative thoughts one step at a time. For example, if you consistently "beat yourself up" about a past decision that you regret, remind yourself, 'I did the best I could with the knowledge that I had at the time.' Or, 'I am human. It is okay to make mistakes. My mistakes do not define me.'

Working through past hurts to unload your wagon can be a challenging process. At any point, do not hesitate to reach out to a counselor or other mental health professional. Talking through your issues with an expert can help bring clarity and give you a healthier perspective on the situation so that you can move forward more easily.

Remember that a large part of keeping a light wagon load is to not allow others to throw their problems into your wagon. Say to yourself, 'This is not my worry or problem. This does not belong to me. I will honor this person by letting them own their own life and choices.' Practice love and compassion but do not let them convince you that their problems are yours to solve. Show them respect by letting them figure out what to do for themselves. You may encourage them and remind them that they will prevail because they have all of the power as Sheriff in their own Me Town. Being fully present when you are listening to them is a gift, as they will feel heard and hopefully understood.

The shared goal for all of us is to be strong. Strong enough to help ourselves become better, one healthy choice at a time. Strong enough to encourage others to be strong. It takes just as much energy to be unhappy as it does to be happy. Thoughts are energy. Put them to good use and lighten your load. Pull the wagon you are proud of and paint it any color you like. Pick the color that says, 'Nothing can break me now.' You have all the power you need to pull your wagon, Sheriff. Run your town with less burden and you will have more energy, happiness, friendship, compassion and harmony in your life.

Self-Reflective Questions:

Do I need to feel love? Do I love myself?

_____
_____
_____

Do I need to forgive myself for a choice that wasn't very good?

_____
_____
_____

Do I need or want to forgive someone else?

_____
_____
_____

Do I need to apologize and ask someone to forgive me?

_____
_____
_____

Do I need to let go of someone in my life who is not healthy for me?

_____
_____
_____

Do I need to let go of something I cannot control (e.g., other people and other situations)?

_____
_____
_____

Do I need to be kinder or more patient with myself and others?

_____
_____
_____

CHAPTER 2

What Are the Laws in Me Town?

As Sheriff of Me Town, you enforce the laws, however, before you can enforce them you must first learn the laws. You determine the type of horse you will hitch your thoughts to. Will it be gentle and obedient or aggressive and wild? You choose what boots to wear and how well you will keep them clean. Will they be the right size for your foot or too skinny and short? If you accidentally lock yourself up in jail, you have the keys in your pocket at all times and the ability to free yourself. Will you give yourself the gift of forgiveness and hence the key to finding freedom from shame? As you work through the issues that may arise, it's important that you learn to release any distractions and how to let them go, because you can. These are just some examples of the type of laws and situations you'll be faced with. Becoming Sheriff of Me Town requires the ongoing practice of taking responsibility for who you are and what you do. As Sheriff, you need to make some decisions about what you will allow in your town. Keep in mind, Me Town is all about you creating a new world for yourself that allows you to create a place that keeps out anything or anyone that disrupts your space. This may seem difficult at first, but I am with you on this journey and I won't let you give up.

Now is a good time for you to think about who you are going to allow to ride into your town. Will you admit only folks inside that love you? Will you allow entrance to only those who treat you with dignity and respect? You can keep bullies out by making sure your emotional, mental, and physical boundaries are in place. Identify those people who should be kept out – like an angry selfish neighbor or an unfair superior. If they are dangerous, they should not be allowed to visit your emotions. To evict them you may have to talk to them from across your border. You can choose to be detached and deal with them on an as-needed intellectual or physical basis only.

Go to jail...go directly to jail is the message you deliver to those nasty self-defeating thoughts that creep into your mind before you even know they have arrived in Me Town. Ask yourself, 'What do I need to lock up in my jail? Do I have resentiments, loathing, regrets, and any other beliefs that cause agitation in Me Town?' After you answer these questions begin to recognize how those negative beliefs affect you. Now ask yourself, 'How do I run those unsavory characters out of Me Town and keep them out for good?' You have all the power to do just that. Agitation station is a state of mind that remains under lock and key and is not free to roam. Access is denied by the Sheriff.

Every town must be governed by laws to maintain order. Chaos in Me Town, like the aforementioned gunfights and bank robberies, symbolize your inner turmoil and pain that leave you feeling powerless. When you take over as Sheriff, you must implement rules to stop the chaos and put yourself back in control. Repeat these laws to yourself, and feel free to add laws that you feel will make Me Town even better.

Law #1
I will remember that I have all the power. I believe I am strong and that helps me to feel strong. I will repeatedly say to myself, 'I can do this.'

What can you do to develop your confidence? Positive self-talk and being your own best cheerleader as a way of life is a good strategy. However, it is taking risks that facilitate our ability to feel self-assured and powerful. Can you think about something you have done in your life that has helped you feel stronger about yourself, a moment that you are genuinely proud of? A personal example is when I started working for the City of Albuquerque. In my position, I realized I was going to be required to do a lot of training of employees as an essential function of my job. I did not have this type of experience in my holster and I felt unqualified. Then one day while I was on the elevator, I saw a poster on the bulletin board for a group called "Toastmasters." It advertised helping people learn how to have confidence in making presentations. I wrote down the information and attended the meeting. I was delighted to discover everyone there was also a city employee, so I immediately felt like I was a part of this team. During the meeting, we were required to prepare and present ten speeches in which the moderators handed out an outline for the type and how long the speech was supposed to last to become a competent toastmaster or a CTM as they referred to it. I was not sure what a CTM was, but I knew if it had the word "competent" in the title I would certainly feel that way.

Over the course of almost a year, I attended weekly meetings and listened to other members make their presentations. Everyone in the room was invited to give feedback about how they were affected by the speech and gave concrete pieces of advice based upon how they were impacted either by the message, body language, vocal tone, eye contact, passion for the subject and what might have made it more memorable. Additionally, someone in the group was responsible for recording how many times the speaker said "Um" and "Ahh" and "So" and other fillers that take away from the message and what amounts to a spot on delivery without hesitations. The speaker was allowed a certain amount of time to present their speech and if they went over that time, they were not allowed to say another word. Every week we would have a practice run and a few of us were asked a question and we had to answer it in 60 seconds. The goal was to develop confidence in spontaneity, knowing your mind and presentation of self. For example, a question might be, 'So Julia, what do you think about what is happening to our country based upon the protests and unrest that have been happening in our streets?' I was given a few seconds and then ready, set, answer the question with confidence and poise. I became geared up for whatever anyone might ask me before or after a presentation, not to mention growing to enjoy the actual opportunity to present to folks something I thought was important and could potentially improve their lives. I became a "Competent Toastmaster," with the help of the people in my club who cared enough about me and themselves to become a better speaker. If I had decided to go to lunch with friends instead of taking the risks, doing the work and summoning my courage at these weekly meetings for almost a year, I would not be the confident speaker I am today. I developed my confidence because I wanted to have it, I wanted to change. I said to myself, 'I can do this.'

Law # 2
I will recognize that my relationship with myself is the most important one I have. My priority is to guide and nurture myself. I will live my life so that when I reach the end I will say, 'I enjoyed that.'

We are kind to ourselves when we decide that we are going to take pleasure and find amusement in life from within. How do you enjoy life? You can be your own best guide by learning from yourself and others, allowing their examples of how to accomplish and how to love life, help you. One example of learning from others is to read the obituaries and find out what it was people enjoyed and will be remembered for. I read the obituaries almost every day to find out what treasures we have lost in my community, and how they lived life to the fullest. It inspires me to learn about what, at the end of their journeys, they are going to be remembered for and what they enjoyed. Everyone has unique interests, pleasures, and passions, so make sure you know and embrace yours and are having as much fun as possible, no matter what you happen to be up to.

I remember as a child, once a year, I would help my father take down the tiny pieces of the glass chandelier above the dining room table piece by piece and wash them in soap and warm water. I would be his loyal assistant in this venture, and carefully transport the pieces to the sink after he handed them to me. He would come down from the ladder and carefully wash them in the soapy water, rinse them and hand them to me to dry with a soft cloth. When we were all done with the first part of our job, we would have a drink and a snack to refresh ourselves from this hard work. It took much concentration so fatigue would set in because if one piece was broken it would not be the same chandelier. It was fun because we made it fun, we enjoyed completing this project every year. We had a great time being together and making our home a cleaner, nicer, more beautiful place to be. When we had nourished ourselves and had more than one laugh, it was time for him to climb back up on the ladder where I would deliver the sparkling clean pieces of cut glass back to him two at a time, and he would carefully replace them. I remember I was glad I was not the one who had to remember which piece went where! Enjoying what you are doing, whatever that may be is the key to enjoying your life. It is you who can make it so, Sheriff.

Law # 3
I will not allow others to disrespect me. I will not tolerate bad behavior and when I feel disrespected, I will say out loud, 'Stop that! or 'Stop talking!' I will explain the type of behavior that is not allowed and announce, 'It is not okay to speak to me this way.' Or 'Your words are hurtful, and it is not okay to hurt me, ever.'

Laying down this law is vital to your well-being, self-esteem and protecting the core of who you are. Take precaution, if you are with someone who is also hurting you physically, you may need people with you before you can say it safely. That may be a mediator, a supervisor, a friend, any natural support you have, or sometimes it may require a security officer or the police. The point is once you let someone disrespect you, chances are they will do it again. Unfortunately, some people will try to crush your spirit and control you. Remember this does not happen by accident, and it may happen again and again before you realize what has occurred. That's okay, sometimes we can be shocked into silence because we cannot believe what someone else has just said to us. Don't worry Sheriff, you've got this now.

Law # 4
I will have a good time being alive. I will pay attention to what is happening with my body and mind. I will stay out of my imagination and really experience what is going on around me right now, in this present moment.

Life is really fun when you have made the firm decision to enjoy it. This state of being is accomplished by being in alignment with the present. Pay attention and if something feels uncomfortable or is hurting, stop what you are doing and fix it. This may include a physical, emotional, spiritual, social or sexual response.

Physical sensation: 'Why does my leg hurt?'

Emotional reaction: 'That felt like a slap in the face.'

Spiritual reaction: 'Why do I feel like I'm in hell?'

Social reaction: 'I do not want to spend time with this person.'

Sexual misstep: 'I am going to stop this now.'

If you are aware of what is not bringing you joy, you can make an educated decision and change the record. Do not make up a story and convince yourself that everything is okay when it is not! Be real with yourself Sheriff, and implement the law of having a good time as often as possible while you are alive. Allowing falsehoods in Me Town will drag you away from the great life you deserve, as well as time well spent.

Law # 5
I will remember that loving other people leads to much joy and great reward. But if I need to end a relationship because it is unhappy and/or unsafe, I will do so. I owe that to myself.

Breaking up is hard to do, just listen to the songs on the radio. Most of us have this history in common, and if you need to end a relationship there are a variety of strategies to make this happen. Do not hesitate to end a relationship out of fear that you will be alone and miserable for the rest of your life. There are beautiful, fun, hilarious, creative and giving people all around you. Get to know them.

Law # 6
I will be honest about creating my suffering. I must accept that sometimes when I feel rotten, it is because I have forgotten that I am in charge of my thoughts.

This is a big law to swallow. Practice, practice, practice, owning this as the truth. You have all the power to believe whatever you want. Make it your practice to be generous with yourself by thinking about life in a proactive manner, generating thoughts that make you feel good about yourself. Come up with a wide variety of positive self-affirmations and discover interesting topics to explore. Take a trip to shake up your headspace, even if it is only a short road trip to someplace you have never visited.

Law # 7
I will forgive myself when I break my own Me Town laws. I will make new ones to build my strength and confidence. My thoughts are my ammunition to feel powerful and at peace, and to recognize in each moment that I am free. I am Sheriff.

Every time you decide to make a new law or amend a current law in Me Town, it becomes a learning opportunity. You are your power and your power is you. What do you want your laws in Me Town to look like, behaviorally? If they influence and guide you to know what you want for yourself, this is in your control to decide. You are now the grown-up in the room. To mess up is part of being human, it is how we learn that the choice we made was not a good one. The good news is you are in charge of making your Me Town laws. If one is not working for you, perhaps it needs to be reworded or amended so you can be friends with it and make it your own. Mistakes are miscalculations. You are smart, you will do better next time. Step into your power with your Sheriff of Me Town laws.

CHAPTER 3

What do You Value as Sheriff?

Who you are, and how you make your decisions, are heavily influenced by your values. Values include the qualities and principles that you hold dear. Honesty and kindness, for example, are standards of how to behave and how to treat others. When making choices about something we want or whether to take a certain action our values are always a factor. They help us determine not only what is important to us but prompt us to consider how our decision might affect others. It is crucial to have a deep understanding of who you are as Sheriff of Me Town, what is important to you, and what values you choose to live by as you make decisions. As you go through life your perspective changes, and so can your priorities. It is important to "check-in" with yourself every so often, to recognize how you or your perspective may have changed, and how your values now apply.

Identifying what you want requires revisiting the characteristics and qualities essential to generating your self-awareness, e.g., reflection about who you have become up to this point in your life. Do this consistently so you know who you are right now and so you are not operating from a frame of reference of who you used to be. We all have a tendency to use habitual ways of thinking and patterns of behavior that we become comfortable with. The challenge is to step out of your comfort zone and look at who you are with a fresh perspective, which will allow you the opportunity to better understand yourself and to have deeper relationships with others.

So, what do you want? As previously mentioned, what we want is different from what we need. Needs are the requirements and necessities for living; food, water, shelter, connection to a purpose or person, elements we must have to survive. What you want is what you crave, long for, desire most, what makes you feel complete.

I want you to take a look at two different examples below of how different values affected the type of lives that were lived. One patient, who I will call Sharon was unable to identify, transform, and create different values from her parents after she experienced childhood trauma. On the other hand, Carla, who also experienced childhood trauma, was able to prevail after deciding at a young age that she was not going to be anything like her parents and she would become a loving parent based on what she observed in other families and at school.

Sharon grew up in a home that was like a horror movie, only it was real. Her mother was unable to tell her not only where her father was, but also who he might have been. Observing adults shooting heroin and drinking hard liquor right from the bottle, she believed this was how other households were managed until she began kindergarten. She had no friends in her neighborhood as she was not allowed to leave her house except to play in the dirt and make mud pies in her backyard. When she was not watching TV, she was prostituted by her mother to earn money to support her mother's drug habit. One of the men who raped her would bring her candy, and she never forgot this "favor."

I met Sharon who was struggling with ongoing bi-polar disorder with psychosis and had been working as a prostitute. Homeless and addicted to heroin herself, I met her because she was pregnant and needed housing and had recently been approved to receive SSI and food stamps. Unfortunately, her story did not shock me as I was a seasoned counselor with years of trauma work experience. I want to mention my first client with psychosis I worked with in college when I was getting my master's degree in counseling psychology, because it is relevant to this story. I was asked by the university to meet with Jeff because they were considering expelling him and he had to pull himself together or he was going to lose his scholarship. He was an extremely bright individual, he had an abuse history, as well. As we were having our session at the student health center, I noticed he kept looking at the side of my head, turning around in his chair and saying, 'Really cool, really cool.' softly under his breath.

'What is so really cool, Jeff?' I asked him.

He moved closer to me, wheeling forward in his chair that had wheels on it. I started to feel uncomfortable because he had entered my personal space and I knew from the intake notes he had recently been released from jail because of assaulting a guy who lived on his floor in the dorm while he was taking a shower. He looked me right in the eye and exclaimed,

'That new watch you just bought is coming right out of the side of your face!'

The day before I had purchased a new watch because mine was old and couldn't be fixed with a new battery. It was a basic Timex, nothing fancy, but I was rattled not only because he was in my face but because he knew about the new watch. This was the first of many times I have assisted folks with psychotic features who knew information about me that I did not tell them. I am sharing this story with you to set the stage for the following examples.

Now back to Sharon. What made this particular client so memorable was her insight into her inability to value different components in relationships and life such as empathy, compassion and honesty. She was completely forthright about this when I asked her about her plans for her unborn child.

'I don't want it. I'm giving it to an adoption agency the social worker told me about. It deserves better since I don't have no morals and I don't feel love.'

I looked at her and said, 'Believing your baby deserves more than what you can provide for her is a trait of a caring person.'

Sharon looked at me and let out a hearty laugh. 'I don't care about this thing inside of me, that was an accident and I waited too long to get rid of it. My mom hated me, and I hate it. When I feel it move I want to hurt it but if I do that I'll hurt myself so I'm not doing that.'

As we continued to talk, Sharon believed for as long as she could remember that her role in life was to use other people, lie to get whatever she wanted, commit a crime, and stay high every moment of every day as often as she could, period. She was not interested in being any different, she was perfectly satisfied with herself. Right before our session ended, she cocked her head and looked at me with a frown.

'Just because you bought yourself a house don't make you no better than me, you bitch,' she said.

I had just signed the mortgage papers on my new house that morning. I leaned forward and said to Sharon before she got up and slammed my door to my office,

'I don't believe I am better than you, Sharon, just a hell of a lot luckier.'

For whatever reason I cannot explain, I have met dozens of clients who can "read" me. I had a supervisor tell me once it is because I am so genuine and transparent when I give unconditional positive regard for people during our counseling sessions. It was a good answer and I liked the compliment but I have never been sure that it is accurate since the coincidence is what they have in common, a diagnosis of psychosis. I give love to my clients regardless of what they say or do, this is just an interesting aside that has been a constant during my career that will also be included in the next story about Carla.

Carla grew up in a home that was like a horror movie, only it was real. Her mother had Schizophrenia with both paranoid and psychotic features. Her father left the home when Carla was just an infant. She had no siblings, and her mother's family had nothing to do with their bizarre daughter, sister and niece. For as long as she could remember, Carla was forbidden to go outside to play with other children. She did attend school but had strict orders to come home directly with no outside activities allowed. No matter how much she begged her mother about joining Girl Scouts or singing in the choir, it was always a resounding, 'No! It is not safe on the outside. You will be tortured and murdered if you disobey me! Now shut up and go to your room.' There was a television in the home, but she was only allowed to watch it with her mother when her mother wanted to watch a specific program.

Not surprisingly, Carla developed a multiple personality disorder. She would make up friends in her mind to play with and they ended up sticking around to become both her cheerleaders and tormentors. She was actively psychotic most of the time but learned to turn down the volume on the voices when conversing with others practically all of the time. When

I met Carla, she had come to me for advice about dealing with a co-worker who was bullying her. Yes, she was not only employed but had two children and a husband. When I asked what she enjoyed about being a mother, she smiled and replied,

'I love being a grizzly bear for my kids. No one is going to hurt them because of me. I let them do all the things they want to do at school and in our neighborhood, I want them to be free and know about people. It has been hard for me but I learned from my teachers and books growing up all the different choices you can make to raise a good kid. A grizzly bear momma will take care of it, and my kids know that.'

I was deeply moved by the tenacity, sheer will-power, and strength this woman had developed pretty much on her own, except for the caring teachers at school who helped her and could tell as a child she needed some extra attention in the human development department.

I replied, 'Carla, you are probably the very best grizzly momma on the planet! I am in awe of you! Now how can we use that grizzly spirit in helping you confront this bully?'

Tears welled up in her eyes and she said softly, 'Between your grizzly spirit and mine I know we can do it. And one of the others just told me, you like the grizzly bear who lives in **_your_** house.'

The others are how she referred to the other personalities who lived in her head. My jaw dropped. The previous weekend I had hung a grizzly bear picture with inspiring words on the bottom of it, on the wall of my garage. I collected myself and said,

'I am here for you. We will figure this out and circle the wagons with your manager's help. I know him and he will not tolerate this.'

I use these two examples that both seem so similar in their foundational values, however, their choices in life have been on the opposite sides of the spectrum. Why did these women have such different personalities? I believe it is because one developed and practiced values and one did not. Values developed and practiced by a person so wounded could have pushed Carla to choose to commit suicide and give up not only because of painful memories and abuse from her mother but the constant distraction of living in her mind with several other personalities. However, on the contrary, she wanted nothing more than to be a good mother with the values of family, love, and the gumption to stand up for herself and ask for help dealing with a disrespectful person. I held in my heart deep respect for this client and her resiliency.

When I walked into my home after work that night, I went out to the garage and looked at that picture again. I looked at it differently from that day forward.

Knowing what your values are will make Me Town a more comfortable, welcoming and authentic place for you. You can appreciate knowing that you have learned what values look like as you have hopefully witnessed and learned from others putting them into practice, which makes you quite fortunate. Values are not considered important by some people and therefore the practice of ethics, morals, and setting codes of behavior for oneself is not a universal mission. Part of knowing and appreciating that you have values is practicing gratitude for the life you have and all of the changes that have occurred around you that have worked out in your favor. Remember, everything in the universe is constantly changing, expanding, shrinking and moving. You are part of this simmering pot of stew, and you do not want to become stuck on the bottom.

When it comes to your values you must also accept that what is treasured and important to you may not be acknowledged nor respected by those around you. If practicing values is not a part of their purpose, this fact will become clear to you either quickly or over time. Regardless, the old Missouri expression, 'You can't expect more than a grunt from a hog,' will make you smile and help you distance yourself from people who do not value you as a person, an equal and an individual who is worthy of all that is good. Stay away from these folks as they have a tendency to cherish only themselves. Their values lie in self-absorption and certainly not the generosity of spirit because they have nothing to give you.

Whatever you see as your current goal in life will help you clarify what it is you value, and help you make better decisions. As you travel through life, you will have a variety of missions, often at the same time. Creating a mission statement for your life that aligns with your values will help you reach the goals of Me Town. You can create a mission statement for yourself by the hour, the day, the week, the year, or your lifespan. Sometimes the goal is simply to breathe calmly while dealing with a momentary stressful situation. Others are larger in scope, like I will be a good guardian of my money and avoid going to the casino. All are important. The goal is to remember what direction you want to be pointed in so you can hit the bullseye on a daily basis.

Once you create your mission statement, stay focused on your mission. It is empowering to realize that each moment is within your control. The more powerful you can feel in terms of being in control of what you want to accomplish and what is in your best interest, the wiser the choices you will make for Me Town. Chance will throw you curveballs, so be ready. What you want will change, so check in with yourself frequently about what your current mission is so that your energy and efforts are put toward your actual desired goal. Be careful not to assume you know what someone else's mission is. Crossing those boundaries is almost like looking in someone else's wallet, purse or looking at the history in their phone. Keep your eyes on your prize, Sheriff, and if others want to share with you what their missions are, terrific. A mission for oneself is like your medical chart; highly personal with a history to back up current choices, behaviors and plans.

Examining your life is a good reminder that we are all just visiting this Earth, and today could be our last. This is one more reason to get focused and live with concentrated intent rather than lumbering along without much thought about our choices or our lives. How did you live, Sheriff? What is your legacy? I know for myself I want to be remembered for my generosity of spirit, love, time, money and giving my smile and laughter to put a shine on the day and deliver joy to another person's heart. I want to be remembered for the things I value and being strong enough to love people and get out of my preconceived notions of whether or not they deserved kindness because everyone deserves kindness no matter how unlikeable they may be. This is about my willingness to give and not their worthiness to take – also known as unconditional love. I am most grateful I have had so many opportunities to practice this as a counselor, consultant and human being.

Take a few minutes to have some fun with the following exercises for some insight into who you are today.

What do you value as Sheriff, and why? Create a list of ten values/qualities you hold dear, that you want to enjoy in Me Town. If you can come up with ten quickly, generate ten more. If you struggle to come up with ten, take time to contemplate what is important to you. What will bring you joy and ignite your passion? What will make Me Town an even better place? Why is this important to you?

_____
_____
_____

What do you want to accomplish? What is your task, your purpose here on Earth? To help others? To feel less anxiety? To reach a certain career goal? To experience life with an open mind and an open heart? To surround yourself with loving family and friends? Write your mission statement.

_____

_____

_____

How do you want to be remembered? Write your obituary and see if your vision of how you will be remembered corresponds with your values and how you currently live your life. As you write, consider these questions: How did you approach your life? Did you try to live the values that were important to you? How did you treat others (loved ones, friends, strangers)? What do you think their perception of you will be? What do you want their perception of you to be? Did you accomplish some or all of the missions you set out for yourself? Were you satisfied overall with the life you had?

Consider how obituaries are written in the newspaper as a guide to writing your own. Be honest and bold. Write it for you and if you want, for the people in your life whom you love. If you are on a roll, write your epitaph as well – what you would want to be engraved on a cemetery headstone or memorial plaque?

Now that you have some current insight into who and how you are, here are some thoughts you can say to yourself or speak out loud privately to yourself to help you stay calm as you make decisions:

'I am in charge of me and no one can take my freedom away. I will decide what to do based on how my choice will make me stronger, happier, and more content.'

'This is making me smile with my heart and my eyes. I am being true to myself.'

'I wear the power badge of Sheriff on my chest with honor and respect for myself. I practice compassion and recognize that everyone makes mistakes, including me.'

'Some people will need to be escorted out of Me Town because they make too much trouble here. My physical and emotional safety are my most important priorities.'

CHAPTER 4

Own Your Decisions, Sheriff

Making a decision is about taking action and owning up to the consequences. As Sheriff of Me Town, you are responsible for making up your mind about something and concluding that you are taking the best action. When you are decisive you can make statements such as, 'This is going to be what I do for myself because I believe this is the healthiest choice I can make for me.' Whatever you do, do not base your decisions on what you believe other people might think. Let their actions and reactions belong to them. Be conscious of what your choices are and why you make them. Understand "why" and "how" you conclude your choice was the wisest decision you could have made for yourself. If you choose to live happily and bravely, you must actively make decisions that support that as your best interest. After you begin owning your decisions as Sheriff, you will feel good about being decisive.

We make decisions every day, some of them are as simple as: 'What do I want to eat for breakfast? Is it too late in the day to drink more coffee because it keeps me awake when I drink it past 3 pm? Am I going to read this book tonight or dance in the living room to oldies Motown with my spouse? Should I cut my hair short?'

Bigger decisions hold more significant consequences. Examples of bigger decisions include life-altering questions such as, 'Should I get pregnant?' Making a decision that major means you will need to do a thorough introspection as to how the consequences will affect your life as this commitment will last a lifetime. You will need to be honest with yourself, is this a decision you are making because you want to or because you feel pressured? Before making such a huge decision, I would suggest you gather more information from books written by other women who have been down that road. It would be a good idea to contact your physician or your most trusted natural supports and gather the information that can help support you and your decision. Unlike choosing to drink coffee late in the day, rearing a child includes constant devotion, mentoring and sacrifice.

Let me warn you, big decisions based on emotions or feeling "pressured" are typically not coming from a clear mindset where you weigh all of your options. Think about how many women decide to get pregnant because they are being pressured by the biological ticking time clock or because their loved ones pressure them. Deciding to please others goes against what decision-making needs to look like in Me Town. In this case like many other big decisions, it cannot be reversed. The same introspection will apply to any situation.

The goals in your decision-making are about doing what is going to please you, make you feel healthy, and shape who you are right now. There should be confidence in knowing you are doing something that you want to do, this is vital to obtaining the outcome you desire. When you feel decisive you will feel firm, determined and purposeful.

Little decisions you may make lightly, big decisions you may make intensely. I suggest having a solid approach for processing your decision to ensure you are thinking each decision through. One method is to incorporate a pro/con list with much consideration. In case you haven't used a pro/con list before, this is a simple way to get your thoughts from your head onto paper. I suggest this simple method of writing Pro (or why is this good for me/us/them) on the top part of the piece of paper and draw a line down the middle. On the opposite write Con (or why is this not good for me/us/them) and underneath each heading list the reasons why your decision does or does not meet the components necessary for you to consider it is a good goal/plan. Once your list is done, you will have a template of what to do and proceed with confidence because you have created a plan towards good decision-making. Other people like to take a hike to get perspective, some folks may smoke or drink medicine that temporarily alters perspective and leads to new insights. Others will go into their deepest spiritual place and use teachings and different wisdoms from a wide variety of teachers to create vision and wisdom of their own. The lesson is take a goal and look at what you want and need with all of the fresh acumen and awareness you can muster.

This isn't going to be easy. Big decisions often require a great deal of stress to fuel your sense of urgency to decide with conviction. However, you must believe you can trust your judgement and avoid self-doubt. Being decisive means marching forward, knowing you have weighed potential outcomes, measuring the potential consequences. Take a stand as Sheriff. Not everyone is going to like or even honor your decisions. That is unfortunate for them. You did not make your decision for them, you made it for you and your well-being. You have all the power. You must also be flexible about the decision you make and allow yourself room for error and learning. Once your final decision has been set in motion, down the line it may need to be amended or even withdrawn.

There was a client who came to see me who had made a decision with deep thought and conviction four years prior. He asked for my help with managing his stress and anxiety. He could not figure out why he had this annoying twist in his gut throughout the day that he could not get rid of, no matter how many miles he ran or heavy weights he lifted. He described himself as a light drinker, a good sleeper and he loved his job. He had a healthy social life with friends he still hung out with occasionally from childhood that were like his brothers, and he was also close to members of his family of origin. He was agnostic in his spiritual beliefs but when he went running in the mountains with the trees and wildlife, that became his temple of worship. When asked about finances he described himself as "frugal to a fault." Nope, it was this "curse," this chronic anxiety, he just could not shake. He was adamant he did not want psychotropic medications to lift his mood or quiet his mind. 'I'm a health nut!' he exclaimed. After about 30 minutes of assessment, I asked him,

'Do you share a home with anyone?'

His eye contact left mine for the first time and he looked at the clock on the wall.

'I need to get back to work pretty soon, so if you have any books or handouts that would be good.'

It does not take a licensed counselor to figure out this was a topic he wanted to avoid, translated this is probably an important clue to helping the client fearlessly name the problem. I waited for his answer in silence.

'I have lived with my girlfriend for about ten years. We keep our finances separate and she is a vegetarian and does yoga. It is good.'

I found this answer to be without passion for his lover, not to mention friendship or mutual respect. So I probed a bit,

'What is it that you love about her? Ten years is 25% of your life so far. Tell me about your relationship.'

He repositioned himself in his chair and lowered his voice, speaking very softly,

'I don't really tell anyone but my lover is another guy. Call me old fashioned but it is private and don't want it to be a "thing" you know what I mean? We are liberals because we swing…you know, sleep with other people. So I'm not *that* in the closet! We decided a few years ago to spice up our sex lives, so when we meet someone we want to have sex with, we know that we can.' He smiled a tiny bit.

'So how is that working for you?' I asked him, using the same soft voice he had been using.

I do not think a second went by before he groaned, shouted a series of expletives, and grabbed the box of tissues sitting next to him. Sobbing uncontrollably for a few minutes, he gathered himself until he could speak,

'I came home from work early to surprise him with concert tickets and a bottle of wine, and I found him having sex in our bed with one of our closest friends! I lost it, ran out to my car and sideswiped the entire right side of his truck. I felt so sick like I wanted to drive myself to the hospital and tell the ER I'm dying inside, but what was I going to say? My boyfriend is a whore?!'

This is an example where a serious past decision was made during the relationship and after four years of engaging in the new custom, it was not working anymore. Apparently, it was time to reevaluate and discover if a new decision around sexual boundaries needed to be made. What did this couple decide to do? I will keep that part of the story completely private, because the best outcome was for them to decide, not us peeking in on a serious personal relationship crisis. The point here is sometimes changes need to be made from experience, and original plans for happiness occasionally need to be altered because the original decision isn't healthy or desirable anymore.

In Me Town, you should strive to make a conscious effort to decide how you will think and behave rather than living out of habit or fear. Be careful using excuses like, 'This is just the way I am. This is how I am supposed to be. This is what others expect me to do. At least I know what I am dealing with in the current situation.' Me Town deserves a decisive Sheriff. When making an important decision, be as thoughtful as you can in your approach. Also, remember that even the best decision, may not result in the outcome you planned because of forces outside of your control. Truthfully, everything is out of your control except for what you think. Life happens and you must be flexible. Take the pressure off of yourself by recognizing that depending on the situation, your decision does not always have to be final. Go ahead and meditate on this for a moment. I also want you to write down on a piece of paper the following statement,

'I have the right to change my mind about this in the future.'

Now take a deep breath. It is time to take action.

The best decisions in the world are wasted if a person does not put their choice into action. Taking action is the embodiment of owning your power. It may be a risk, but every person must take risks to be able to live fully. Play to win but also recognize that nobody wins all of the time. See the value in taking chances and learning from the outcomes. The more you practice this, the stronger you become. Then, when the time comes to make an enormously challenging decision, you will have made friends with the process and be more confident and decisive. Don't be afraid to go for it, Sheriff. Me Town needs your leadership. If you are a person that has difficulty in this area, you are not alone. I have listed key strategies below to help you become a more confident decision maker. Use this as a guide when faced with a major decision.

Decision-Making 101:

- Identify the specific decision you need to make. How significant is it? Will this decision change your life or someone else's life in a major way? Or is it less impactful, albeit important?

- Identify and assess your options. Write down each possible decision, along with the potential consequences of each. Think about the long-term as well as the short-term implications. Ask yourself, 'If I was giving myself the best possible outcome as a result of this decision, what would it be?'

- Do not make your decision based on "should." The only duty and obligation you have to yourself are to live well and be well. That means you value the condition of your mind, body and spirit.

- Consider your values. Make the choice that reflects what is true and right for you and gives you peace of mind.

- Identify what you want. Why does this problem need to be solved? When you clearly understand why this decision is important to you, you will be able to determine what is best.

- Examine the potential consequences of your decision once you are close to making your choice. Make sure you can live with them if one of them were to become reality. It may be unpleasant, but if you can live with the consequence, it could possibly be your best choice.

Make a commitment to yourself that you will be intelligent and confident when making a decision that is being witnessed by others. Do not "play it small" to accommodate people who may be negatively reacting to your capable decisiveness. Sometimes others will react to your certainty with, 'Are you sure?' or 'Maybe we should talk about this some more so I can give you my opinion.' One example of dealing with these folks is by replying, 'No, I am certain and this is my decision. Thanks for your interest.' Other times may require you walking away so your boundary becomes established. Either way, you are an accomplished decision-maker and powerful beyond measure. Do not give the naysayers your attention, because consciously or unconsciously they are attempting to instill self-doubt in your mind.

CHAPTER 5

Your Words Are Your Path, Sheriff

Did you know you speak roughly 16,000 words each day? Are you aware of what you are saying? Do you know what you mean when you speak, and the impact that it may have on those who hear it? Do you want to understand yourself and others better, and communicate clearly? If you answered yes to these questions, you are extremely focused, considerate and wise beyond measure. Please keep up these strengths and values and take pride in being one of the few people who communicate better than most of us. Thank you for being a role-model, and know most of us are listening to you as our example.

So how can our words help us become a better Sheriff? Once again, think about what kind of town you want to run. Do you want to run a peaceful town, remembering that you can't take back whatever comes out of your mouth or do you impulsively speak out with words that may harm yourself or others? How you speak to and about yourself, and those in your life, sets the tone for how you run Me Town.

Keep in mind that you own the road paved by your words, Sheriff. The words you use create your reality. Your words create your story. The more creative you are when you use a variety of words, the more you value broadening your vocabulary, the smarter your mind will become and the more information you will have to help you run Me Town. The tools to facilitate creativity are words, languages, reading information that is unfamiliar to you, spending time with active and exploratory minds, brainstorming some original thoughts, and having the motivation and energy to figure out how things work, also known as being inventive. Take the initiative to create new visions for yourself, and plan a daily practice of using your words to create a new plan for talking to yourself and others about what used to be mundane but is now renewed and celebrated. It is fun to write down something you are used to thinking about in a certain way and turning it upside down so it now seems very different. Step out of your word box and enjoy the new path where your reorganized thinking can take you.

Choosing your words carefully helps you to convey your message clearly so that it is understood correctly by others. This gives you more clarity about who you are, and more power in your day-to-day life. Everyone wants to be heard and understood. Communicating authentically about who you are, what you need, what you want and what you do not want or will not allow in your life, is the mark of a strong, honest Sheriff.

Sometimes, it is hard to find the right words to say what is in your mind and heart. You might need some clarification on the best words to get your point across. When you need some help, turn to the tried-and-true dictionary. Consider it your faithful, trusty steed – the horse you can ride with confidence to carry you from confusion to clarity as you speak your mind.

The better understanding you have of using your mind, senses and gut feelings will also help you become a much better active listener. It is a gift to another person when you are a good audience, and when you listen to their words, their story and sincerely believe at that moment, it is the most important conversation you have ever had. When you are attending to another person's message, they know you are hearing them because of your body language, responses, and mere silence without interruption as they describe to you what is happening to them. Even when you are with someone who talks pretty much constantly about themselves or other topics they are visiting, showing no interest in nor questions about you, it is important to pay attention so you may politely exit the vicinity and move on. Some people talk incessantly as a coping mechanism out of fear of what you or anyone else for that matter, may say. Others are self-absorbed and in love with the sound of their voice and words. These folks abound and it is important to spend as little time with them as possible because they are not going to change, most likely, unless they have an epiphany as to why interesting people do not want to hang out with them. Personally, I prefer to be engaged as an equal in my relationships and not used as a recording device. If someone is not interested in a mutual exchange of words to build our relationship upon, then I know we will not have a relationship but I will become an expert about everything that means something to *them.* Even in a counseling relationship, my ability to speak and express myself is important to the therapeutic relationship because I am there as an expert and consultant. If a client is not willing to listen to my feedback then we are both wasting our time. In terms of family and friends, if I cannot nudge the person towards curiosity about me, I do not spend much time with them. It's not enjoyable, rewarding, and can be downright exhausting soaking up every detail that is not my life, but theirs on a buffet table they expect me to eat. I will not be there; I am not that hungry for listening to people's verbal takes on whatever pops into their minds without focus or consideration for their audience. I am a giver and a big piece of that identity is I need other people in my personal life who can give back to me. An equal word exchange is deeply important to a satisfying human connection. Let's talk some more about the importance of words.

Become smarter and wiser by using and understanding definitions that bring meaning to your life. Become a word warrior. This enhanced perspective will help you run Me Town with:

Clarity

How clear and transparent are you when you speak? Do you want to illuminate your message so it and your story are clear? It is a value to speak so others can understand your words. Evaluate if this is a value and if not, I recommend making it one of your most important. That is why you do not use a college-educated vocabulary with someone who dropped out of the 7th grade, they will not understand you. Many people will not ask you to clarify what you are saying because they lack assertiveness skills, believe asking for clarification is rude or they simply got lost in your message and are too embarrassed to ask. It is your responsibility to make sure you are communicating with as much coherence as possible, otherwise, your message will be vague, blurry and easily misunderstood.

Creative Answers to Probing Questions

It can be much fun to practice creativity when there is a question or problem presented by yourself or others and come up with an original idea. When you use your imagination and visualize life quite differently, the possibilities become endless. Use your imagination and words to describe a new invention in problem-solving, deeds and most certainly humor. Some of the funniest jokes and stories arrive because the speaker is ingenious, s/he is clever enough to describe something that breaks the mold of how you are used to looking at it. Hilarious is knowing how to use language (both verbal and nonverbal) to wake up the laughter that you always want to keep near the surface of your personality. Be funny Sheriff, it is amusing, friendly, and endearing.

Patient Self-Understanding

The horseshoe meets the dirt as you ride along the trail and listen to the words you are using with yourself along the way. Remain calm and practice self-restraint before you lose your composure and feel annoyance or even exasperation with yourself. Be aware of your experience (feelings) and avoid being over critical and disapproving of yourself. If you were a jerk, own it and apologize to yourself and others. Be cautious of the ruminating that can go into disparaging yourself, it does not improve anything, it simply is using negative words that are harming your peace of mind. Punishing yourself is stressful, exhausting, grueling and potentially crippling. Understanding is the opposite of the word ignorance. Develop the skill of compassion and goodwill towards yourself by practicing the thoughts that help you arrive in this mindset, 'I am going to be tender, supportive, and approachable while I am focused on who I was, who I am, and who I want to become. I deserve this respect, as do the other people I love in my life besides me. I have made mistakes I have no intention of making again, however, if I do, I will determine how to make a prevention plan for future decision-making so I won't repeat them again and again. This is getting old.' Practice tolerance with yourself, Sheriff and eventually you will become unflappable.

Guidance in Defining What Others May Mean

Embrace your words as your friends; informing your enlightenment when someone else is communicating with you and you just don't get what they mean. Sometimes simply asking a clarifying question will do the trick. However, sometimes the speaker isn't quite sure what they are expressing and this can be a challenge. Always be respectful and understand that not everyone has an issue figured out before they talk about it. The best strategy at times is to say nothing and simply listen, making the goal simply ascertaining what is the message they are trying to give you. Be patient when you are listening to someone who has a stutter, be understanding when conversing with someone whose first language is not English, be compassionate when someone has a developmental delay and can't quite express what they mean. Be kind, smile, and if you just don't get it, just let it go. Have even more energy and desire to be understood by others, and remind yourself that words are a form of power. Power to create understanding, empathy, and simply letting someone know you are here, you are present.

Curiosity

Have you ever had a conversation with someone who seems completely uninterested in what you are saying? It may be communicated through nonverbal behavior such as staring at their phone, yawning, looking through some papers that are not relevant to the conversation, playing with something that is not relevant to the discussion, or verbally without sentences coming out their mouth but just, "Huh" or "Hmmm" or nothing at all. This loud behavior conveys disinterest at best and complete boredom at worst. It is certainly not a powerful reaction to an opportunity to engage. You have no control over how others use their words with you, but you can decide for yourself this is not the rude person I want to be. When engaged use your words to show you are eager to know and digest more. 'Really? Tell me more.' or 'I did not know that, how interesting.' You will soon learn many amazing realities you did not even know existed. This will require you to live with an open, curious value of learning the unknown that includes what other people believe besides you. Use your words to inspire curiosity in yourself and others.

Optimism

Your words you feed your mind also can feed those around you with hope, confidence and good cheer. I have always enjoyed being optimistic because it makes me and others feel good. To feel pessimistic is to be defeated before you have even begun! In times of trouble, it is helpful to find encouragement from others whom you know have the capacity to give this gift to you, to help you remember this too shall pass. When optimism feels light-years away, a few words from yourself and/or others can be the magic pill that delivers you out of the darkness and into the light of truth. What is the light of truth? It is honesty combined with a willingness to remain open to new words and therefore new thoughts, you can and will reinvent yourself. You have done it before and you will do it again, because that is what growth brings to us, as people. It is what the little girl of color does when a mean person calls her terrible and she refuses to believe its negative force and impact, she knows she is good. It is the gay couple holding hands who get spit on by a passing car with hateful words shouted out of the windows, walking on because they know they are good. It is the parent whose son calls him an old, useless idiot and takes a deep breath to find self-control and does so because he knows he is devoted to his troubled, misguided child. He knows who he is, an optimist. 'Words may be hateful but I will not let them rob me of who I am,' an optimist says, who believes the moment will pass, and I am good. 'Words can only hurt me if I take them personally rather than rejecting them as trash.'

Peace of Mind

Once I had a client whose vocabulary consisted of mostly curse words, deprecatory and unflattering snide comments about others including his family, and general cheapening of anything good. He made the darkest, most hateful character in the movies look pretty darn good. He was not in front of me because he wanted to change, but it was a condition of employment because he had violated the violence policy of where he worked and therefore, referred to me to become more civil at work. Within seconds of sitting down in front of me he raised one side of his buttocks and let out a loud sound of passing gas, the loudest fart I believe I have ever heard and I have heard quite a few. I asked him about his family life and he told me all the women in his family know how to work, not sit around doing nothing,

'Like you sitting on that couch all day. They know how to get in there, break a sweat and do stuff!'

Not taking a patient's comments personally is something a good counselor can do in her sleep, and I did not react to this blatant disrespect. After all, it was why he was in my office.

'It sounds like you are really proud of how the women in your family work very hard. What a gift that you respect them so much.'

He leaned forward then crossed his arms. 'Who said anything about respect? They work hard but they are all a bunch of bitches. I almost got in a fistfight last Christmas with my sister when she kept grabbing my son's presents like they were hers, and the only reason I didn't backhand her was because my brother held on to me.'

Bingo. This was a way of life for this client, and I knew the key to successfully treating him was to focus on what he would gain, rather than others. He had zero value for the rights of others to be safe in his presence, physically or emotionally. I asked him if I had a magic wand and could give him anything in the world, what would that be.

'Piece of mind, my blood pressure is through the roof!'

So, we began the work of using his assertive words (rather than curse words, which don't convey needs) to get what he wanted and keep his job. We worked together for several months, and when he was leaving his last session, his graduation as I called it, he turned to me and hugged me.

'You are alright,' he murmured and walked out the door.

I can only hope his piece of mind is making the world a better place.

Acceptance

Refrain from the impulse to go to what may be old familiar expressions that seem like explanations or bring you comfort for what may be difficult to believe or accept, such as; This isn't real! He's a liar behind my back! Why doesn't anybody get me? Life is hard and then you die! Working for a living sucks! Everyone is a user! I never get what I want! If you don't fight you're a chicken! They would have never done this to me had I been stronger!

Words that encourage acceptance of reality and what you have witnessed as true, need to be consciously formulated and then used regularly, so you do not end up with these types of sentences punching you in your cerebral cortex. What may be true may be extremely hard to swallow. Endurance with accepting an event as a fact can be excruciating, but denying it happened will only make life worse. It takes courage to use your words with yourself and others to facilitate acceptance. Take the information and acknowledge it is true (when you are confident that it is) and that it happened. It is only when we use our words of acceptance that you will adopt the occurrence as a reality so you can move on figuring out how you will cope with it. Eventually, you will surrender to the fact that life's difficulties happened and avoid chasing around stories in your brain to ease the pain. It happened. You deny it and you cannot figure out how to move on. You accept it and you begin to heal from the painful reality, the real-life existence. Go to your acceptance file and put in those life lessons that burned you but did not kill you. We have all been there,

Sheriff. Words leading to acceptance of what really happened will give you healing power.

Just like your horse, your words will always help you find your way home.

CHAPTER 6

Run Me Town With Positive Perspective

Oscar Wilde once said, 'To most of us the real life is the life we do not lead.'[1] Sometimes it seems that what we want is just inches away from our grasp. The dream we chase escapes us when we concern ourselves too much with other people's opinions of us as opposed to prioritizing how we spend our time. We can get "caught up"

---

[1] The Book of Positive Quotations, Compiled and Arranged by John Cook copyright 1993, page 71

in running toward the pot of gold at the end of the rainbow, forgetting that the gold is already in our minds.

What does your golden day filled with positive perspective look like? Let's look at two different Sheriffs to illustrate the enormous impact a positive perspective can make in Me Town.

Both Sheriffs own a cattle ranch in the United States, a country where people are free to think and express their thoughts as long as they do not infringe upon the rights and freedom of others. Both are single, in their late 30s, with no children. Both have fairly good health and can see, hear, smell, taste, touch, walk and talk. Neither suffers from severe mental illness. But like the rest of us, both have suffered loss and pain as a result of losing loved ones, as well as through betrayal, deception and people moving on. Like all of us, they are survivors of some type of trauma, and have a few personality defects simply because they are human. What makes them very different from one another are their perspectives, decisions, and the amount of power used to live a golden life, and not a life filled with fool's gold. After reading their stories, you can decide which one owns the goldmine.

It is a Monday morning on both ranches. Let's meet John and Henry, in that order.

John wakes up at 9:30 a.m. and stumbles into the kitchen to make his first cup of instant coffee. He gobbles three chocolate donuts from a box, puts on his jeans, a long-sleeved shirt, and boots, and goes outside to his four-wheeler to check on his herd. He looks at the morning sky and feels that old pain in his heart about how his older brother talked their father into giving all of his assets to the brother who has children "who are going to need it." The hate and resentment he feels for his father and his brother are very strong, and he fantasizes everyday about what his life would have been like if he had inherited the half-million dollars that were his share. John forgets about how happy his mother was enjoying the simple things in life and the beauty all around her on the ranch. He runs over a cactus because he's not paying attention and blows a tire. 'I wasn't made for this kind of life, I deserve better than this!' he yells at the crows who are staring at him and sitting on the fence that needs repair.

John fixes the tire and drives past the sorry-looking garden he planted in the spring. He did manage to harvest a few squash, but he rarely waters the soil and tells himself the cattle are the ones who drink 25-gallons of water a day and that's what he needs to pay attention to. Plus he doesn't like to cook fresh vegetables the way his mother used to for the family because it takes too much chopping. John drives into his four pastures and checks on his 70 head of cattle. Thinking that his back is going to be very sore from unloading hay and feed, he decides to call the neighbor boys to come over and do it for him. They only ask for $180 for the two of them for five hours of work. He figures it is worth it so that he has time to drink some beers before heading into town, then having burgers and more drinks at the tavern, his nightly ritual. He thinks about his girlfriend who left him for another rancher. He has not been willing to love again because he tells himself that, 'Women will just stab you in the back.' He does his best to flirt with the women at the bar before he gets too drunk. He doesn't want to feel lonely anymore. No lady wants to go home with him and he feels angry about that, sometimes resulting in a fistfight with another man outside on his way home.

Around 10 p.m., John will drive home on the back roads in his 20-year-old truck, and if he is lucky he will avoid the cop who always sits at the same intersection on the edge of town waiting for a drunk driver to pass by. He smiles at himself for being so crafty at avoiding the law, falls into bed after taking his boots off, and passes out from the alcohol. He hasn't changed the sheets on his bed since spring because he figures they will just get dirty again anyway. He has about a quarter of a gallon of gas in his tank and tomorrow night on the way to the tavern he will run out of gasoline, be stranded, and curse God for never giving him a break.

Meet Henry

The sun is rising on Henry's ranch. The dim early morning light begins to come into his bedroom window and he wakes up and stretches. He is grateful he has been given another day and then yawns, looking at the sky that rises above his land. He stretches his back and shoulders before rising because he has learned it helps his flexibility and prevents injury while at work. He turns on the coffee pot (he gets it ready before bed as a nightly ritual), and it begins to brew while he picks up his razor and shaves in the hot shower. He fixes his favorite breakfast of three scrambled eggs, toast and jelly, and glances at the picture of his mother he keeps in the kitchen. He shakes his head and remembers how she used to tell him it's not during the good days, but when times are tough that will test how he handles himself as he strives to become a man filled with courage and integrity. She never could have imagined her eldest son, Henry's oldest brother, would have been able to talk her husband out of giving their children equal shares of their assets. Henry feels love for his mother whose voice he heard in his head during that tough betrayal, 'When you trust yourself, son, you have nothing to fear.' Most days he doesn't think about the lies and theft he had no idea his brother was capable of, but he sips his coffee and figures he is thinking about it today because it would have been his mother's 75th birthday. He thinks, *She taught me how to love myself so I could love my life*, as he rises from his breakfast table and heads out the backdoor to his four-wheeler.

Henry drives to his garden and walks among the variety of vegetables that are thriving there. He takes pride in understanding that the quality of the soil is the most cherished ingredient in a successful garden, and he turns on the watering system he installed a few years ago that drips to all of the beautiful food. He met a gorgeous woman at the farmer's market this summer who loves to cook and appreciates using fresh food and herbs he brings to her, which he is harvesting this morning because she has invited him for dinner tonight. He is grateful to be in her presence, for their friendship, and the relationship is blooming. He picks only the finest items for her and knows that pretty smile will be there when he carries the full basket from his truck to her house. He remembers to pick some flowers for her when he is out in the pastures checking on his 110 head herd. He enjoys raising his livestock and is a student and admirer of Temple Grandin; a noted professor of animal science, autism advocate and best-selling author. He respects his cows and has done well in growing his ranch.

After feeding the cattle and making sure they have plenty of water in their troughs, he showers again and puts on a new pair of jeans and shiny Sunday boots to go to dinner. He takes the vegetables, a huge bouquet of flowers he put together, and places a bottle of wine next to him in his new truck, which he was able to purchase with the sale of ten of his steers, which always fetch a great price at the sale barn. He is excited to see the look on her face because her happiness brings him great joy. As he pulls into her driveway he thinks, *This girl just may be the one I marry.* The night is cool with a slight breeze. She opens the front door and throws her arms around him. *This is going to be a great night,* Henry thinks to himself as he walks into her neat-as-a-pin ranch house. This woman has 140 head of cattle herself!

Both men on the same day have the same opportunity to create a life that is rewarding and good. Based on the details described of these two individuals, who do you think is the healthier, happier person? Make no mistake; it is our choices that bring us happiness. How we choose to perceive ourselves, other people and the world is our goldmine. It is the quality of your perceptions that create your feelings and quality of life. Your perceptions are who you are. Recreate them, as needed.

CHAPTER 7

All of Your Choices Are in the Palm of Your Hand

Take your hand and hold it in front of you. Spread your fingers out. Each one is an ever-present reminder of your priorities. When you're feeling lost or overwhelmed, focus on your hand, and know that you are still in control of Me Town.

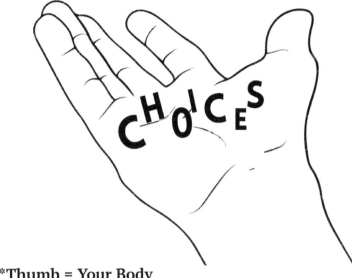

*Thumb = Your Body

Start with your thumb. It represents your body. "Thumbs up" means you are aware of what is going on in your body right now. You are aware of your breathing and other physical sensations. Your gut is calm, your heart feels at peace. You have stretched several times and exercised at least 30 minutes today. You have spent at least 15 minutes in the sunshine, taken your multi-vitamin, and eaten at least five servings of fruits and vegetables, and enjoyed every bite. You have consumed alcohol in moderation. You got a good night's sleep and if not, took a power nap. You have paid attention to your posture and corrected it when you noticed you were slumping. You took your medicine as it was prescribed. You had great sex and it felt like making love because you share your body with a loving person. You used the bathroom and did not hold it. You take care of yourself. You feel alive and energized and at home in your body, so "Thumbs up!" for you, Sheriff.

"Thumbs down" means the choices you are making on behalf of your physical health are not so good for you today. You are feeling some anxiety in your gut and your breathing is shallow and rapid. You ignore your rapid breath and cram as many potato chips in your mouth as you can. You have been sitting in your chair for four hours and have not gotten up once to stretch or use the bathroom. You ignored the urge to use the restroom and picked up the phone instead while looking at the news on the internet. You got home an hour late with a headache and took three aspirin on an empty stomach with about five ounces of bourbon over ice. Still thirsty, you reached for a beer and sat in front of the television. You were too intoxicated to eat food or make love with your partner and s/he went to bed irritated and unsatisfied. You passed out on the couch and woke up at 4 a.m. with another headache and constipation.

Trust your thumb to remind you to take care of your body today and make it a "Thumb up!" day. Celebrate when you have made good choices for your physical being. If you did not choose well, forgive yourself and keep trying; we are all a work in progress.

*Index Finger = Your Mind

Now look at your first finger, often called pointer or index finger. Let it remind you to think like a champion. Place it on your temple and remember the famous phrase, it is the mark of an educated mind to be able to entertain a thought without accepting it. Assess the wisdom of the choices you make every day. Sometimes the best response to life is no response, giving your mind the time it needs to prepare for taking the best care of you. Resist the temptation to react out of habit, and take your time to analyze circumstances and potential strategies before deciding what to do or say. You don't always have to respond to someone or something right away.

Understanding what is right for you and practicing good judgment usually takes a bit of time and reflection. What is conceivable to you now may be an idea, plan, or belief that you would not have been able to formulate five minutes ago. View your brain as a beautiful, strong, and reliable place where you can choose to live in beauty and peace. Be open to learning. Put your index finger on your temple and remember your head is never on lockdown; you are free from the tormenting thoughts and beliefs of the past when you remember that you are a champion of freewill. You have all of the power to think whatever you want.

Here are a few tips for thinking like a champion:

1. Avoid magical thinking. Magical thinking is when you feel that your actions or thoughts can impact something that they have no real control over. For instance, do you remember the saying, 'Step on a crack, break your mother's back?' Magical thinking says that if you actually step on a crack, you fear that you will hurt your mother. Magical thinking can be fun when you buy a lottery ticket, just make sure you don't make financial decisions based upon your belief you will win!

2. Do not be judgmental or become angry when someone else has a different concept of reality. Magical thinking also

includes believing that other people automatically understand you and what you are thinking. They most likely do not.

3. If someone in your life "gets" you, this is special and not to be expected of everyone. Even your most trusted person will not fully understand you, no one can.

4. No one is obligated to understand you. You, however, have an obligation to yourself to persevere and cope with disappointment when misunderstood. It will also benefit you to make the effort to try to understand others.

5. Resist anger when communication becomes difficult. It takes patience and effort to make yourself clear. Be grateful that you have the mental capacity to convey your feelings and thoughts, whether by speaking, writing, moving your body or non-verbal cues.

6. The way out of conflict is through your commitment to growth. Remember you have nothing to prove to anyone except yourself. Be flexible in the ability to change your mind. If you listen to a completely different perspective, you may find all or part of it useful.

7. Become more likable to yourself and others by showing curiosity and interest when someone expresses an opinion that is different from your own. Living with an open mind allows for new ideas and wisdom. Remember even if you treat everyone like gold, that is no guarantee they will be kind to you or love you as much as you love them. Magical thinking says you are good to others so they will be good to you. I wish it were true.

8. Be grateful for the people in your life who have helped broaden your perspective. Thank them. Your expression of appreciation will mean a lot to them and deepen your relationship.

*Middle Finger = Spirit

You now need to look at your middle finger, the longest digit on most human hands.

This represents your spirit – the essence of who you are and the unique energy and aura that you put into the world. Your spirit connects you with the world on a higher level. It guides you when you do not know the truth and nothing seems familiar.

The great truth about choices is that we can make new ones every second and be guided by forces we may not comprehend. How many times have you had a hunch and went with that? How bold are you in listening to your intuition rather than logic? That is your spirit in action, guiding you when you feel lost.

Your spirit is also what moves you when you feel a sense of awe, the power that inspires you. Let yourself be astonished, and marvel at how surprised you can be at any given moment. Place your hand on your heart right now with your middle finger pointing toward your shoulder and say out loud, 'Stay open.' Prevent becoming so self-contained that you block new experiences, discoveries, and passions, from arriving to your heart. When you become tested by life's difficulties, put your hand on your heart and say, 'This, too.' To remind yourself that, 'This too, shall pass.'

Surrender your attempts to control other people or situations and your spirit will grow and give you the freedom to be grateful for your opportunities. Love your spirit and celebrate your freedom to live as if everything you do makes a difference, because it does. You are of this world and what you do matters. You always count. Your spirit is your life force, use it to your advantage and make this world better every moment that you can remember to do so.

*Ring Finger = Your Emotions

Now hold up your fourth finger, which represents your emotions. Notice how this is the most difficult finger to stand at attention on your hand. When this digit is held up all by itself, it provides you with the most individual struggle. This is appropriate, as some of the most challenging obstacles we face in life involve our emotions.

When we are born we enter the world with emotions. As we grow we learn that to a certain extent, we have the ability to self-regulate – to control our feelings and channel their intensity toward positive or negative outcomes.

Our emotions have a direct impact on our body. When you feel joy, fear, anger, or sadness, you make a muscle memory with your body which can lodge anywhere; your gut, forehead, mouth, tongue, hands, eyes, nose, any of your muscles including your heart. If you are uncomfortable with an emotion you are feeling, sometimes it is best to take some deep breaths. Breathe through what you are feeling without judgment and with compassion. Emotions tell us who we are in this instant. Be grateful you can feel them. Many people have become numb to emotion for a variety of reasons. Feel your feelings and trust them as faithful messengers from your body, mind and spirit.

Your ring finger is a reminder to acknowledge your feelings and work through them in a healthy way. Below are some tips to handle some of the common emotions you face.

When Facing Fear

You will inevitably feel fear in Me Town. Sometimes feelings of fear are 100% valid and helpful. You could be in physical danger, or in the presence of someone who is not safe to trust. Fear alerts you to a potential threat, and that awareness can save your life. When facing tangible fears, seek safety first. If you are physically threatened, try to exit the situation and find a safe place to go. With any threat, be as prepared as you can to defend yourself through physical, mental, or verbal means depending on what is appropriate. Steel yourself for "battle." Know yourself well enough to realize when you need back up from others. Tell yourself that as Sheriff, you can handle whatever is coming and that you will be victorious. Fear can keep you alive.

Sometimes fear shows up as feelings of anxiety, and those feelings are your enemy. When we feel anxious, we are usually trying to "slay a dragon" that is not there. We worry about "what ifs" – negative scenarios about the future that we create in our minds, that the great majority of the time never happen. This is our mind's attempt to gain control over things that we are afraid of. When we go to these pretended scenarios we spend physical, mental, and spiritual energy defending ourselves against...nothing. However, generating a scary scenario in our minds that we cannot resolve provokes uneasiness. It can lead to full-blown panic if we do not pull ourselves out of that emotional state. When you are anxious, remind yourself that the imaginary scene playing out in your head is just that – imaginary. It will likely not happen. Distress about future uncertainties can be managed by making a plan with productive strategies. If you have no control over the outcome, concentrate on building skills you do have control over and then let it go. Positive self-talk is always a good soothing technique when it comes to worrying. Coach yourself on all of the reasons you can prevail in life and then move on and get out of your head.

There are different types of fear and different words that describe fearful feelings. When you feel any of the feelings listed below, try to bring your mind back to the present moment.

- Nervous (unnaturally or acutely uneasy or apprehensive).

- Tense (mental or nervous strain; high-strung).

- Worried (to feel uneasy or anxious; torment oneself with disturbing thoughts).

- Afraid (feeling reluctance or unwillingness; filled with apprehension).

- Hesitant (undecided, doubtful, reluctant to act because of fear).
- Alarmed (a sudden fear or distressing suspense due to awareness of danger).
- Panic (a sudden overwhelming fear that produces hysterical behavior).
- Timid (lacking in self-assurance, courage, or boldness).
- Frightened (thrown into a fright; terrified, scared).
- Intimidated (to make timid; filled with fear).
- Jumpy (nervous or apprehensive; jittery).
- Lonely (standing apart; isolated).
- Insecure (doubting; not confident or assured).

Do not allow these feelings to control you. As with all emotions, create an exit strategy where you begin to breathe, contract and relax the muscles in your body, exercise your face, and get back in this moment, which is generally safe. Always remember there is a huge difference between what is, and what could be. Tell yourself that whatever happens, you will be able to handle it. Because you will. This will help you take your power back from your fears.

Anger

When you feel anger, something needs to change. We typically feel anger when life is not going "our way" according to how we see fit. Our angry feelings can be triggered by major or minor developments. Anger is talking to you when your heart rate goes up, your adrenaline and other hormones kick in, and your body temperature and blood pressure rise. It is telling you that you need to take action to change your situation or get out of it altogether.

Everyone gets angry sometimes. When you do, it helps to remind yourself that most people are not trying to harm or slight you, and most situations are not intended to hurt you. Taking things personally greatly exacerbates anger. Try to look at people and life with gentle curiosity and forgiveness instead.

The words below have one thing in common – they are all some form of anger. When we feel these emotions, they can do more damage to us than anyone else.

- Agitated (disturbed, perturbed).

- Annoyed (to bother in a way that displeases or irritates).

- Resentful (to feel or show displeasure from a sense of injury or insult).

- Bitter (showing intense hostility, cynical).

- Envious (to desire something possessed by another).

- Irritated (to excite to impatience or anger, annoy).

- Livid (enraged, furiously angry).

- Critical (inclined to find fault or judge severely).

- Irate (arising from anger).

- Frustration (a feeling of dissatisfaction resulting from unfulfilled needs or unresolved problems).

- Impatient (not readily accepting interference, intolerant, restless in desire or expectation).

- Fed up (disgusted).

When you feel any of these feelings, acknowledge that you are angry, and be clear on exactly what or who is upsetting you and why. Do you have any control over the situation? What can you change about yourself or the circumstances to improve things? If there is nothing you can do, try to accept what is happening and let go of your anger. It is only hurting you. Try not to think of yourself as a victim. Remember – you have already won plenty of battles and proven your strength. You are Sheriff of Me Town. You are powerful.

Sadness

When sad things occur, one person may shrug them off as "life happens." Another becomes weakened to the point of suicide. Emotions ebb and flow, and almost everybody gets the blues. Being melancholy is typical for some, rare for others. Often, that feeling occurs due to an unfortunate event – the death of a loved one, the breakup of a relationship, the loss of a job, etc. Other times, we are sad for reasons that we cannot exactly articulate.

As difficult as it is to experience sadness, it is also a reminder of the joy or good times we were fortunate enough to experience in our life. Acceptance of our sad feelings makes us stronger and helps us to better appreciate who and what we love. Life is fluid, and good things do not always last. When we accept our pain we are honoring the signal that we do indeed have a heart.

Think of your emotions like they are riding on a train (your body). Your mind is the engineer of your train, driving down the track making good choices so you don't run yourself off of the rails. Your imagination is the train station. Sometimes you stop there, get off, and stay until you have tormented yourself long enough, and decide to get back on the train and move forward into real life.

It can be something as simple as a song or an old memory that makes you stop at the imagination station. While you are there, you need to let your sadness out so that you can get back on the train and keep going. Crying is a great way to do this. Letting your tears flow is a natural, healthy way to release the pain from your body. Keeping your sadness inside is unhealthy on every level, physically as well as mentally.

Many people have a hard time allowing themselves to cry, and instead, they withdraw from their normal activities and relationships. They may not show up for the dinner party they said they would attend, or cancel lunches with friends.

If you are so overwhelmed by grief that your tears won't flow, try watching a sad movie or listening to a meaningful song. Often, that will trigger the cathartic release of tears and emotion that you need to be able to start the healing process. If crying is not something you can or want to do, that is okay! As long as you physically do **something** healthy, like working out, beating your hands and arms on a bed, screaming into a pillow. Go ahead and use your imagination and do what feels comfortable for you to let go of the pain.

As you deal with sadness, choose to actively take care of yourself. Give yourself some extra TLC. Watch movies or read books that can comfort you or make you laugh. Get enough rest. Lean on your support network of trusted friends for encouragement and hugs.

If these actions don't help, consider whether you might be experiencing depression. Does it run in your family? Did your Uncle Arthur often "sing the blues" in his life? Was your Great Grandma Martha known to withdraw from the family at times? If so, consider talking with a counselor or psychiatrist. They will be able to help you work through your feelings more easily. And we can all be grateful that antidepressants were invented for those of us who got a bad card and came from a long line of sad personality types. Life is too short to live in misery. There is help out there, and there is no shame in using it to have the happier life that you deserve.

If these words come to mind when thinking about your mood, it is sadness that you are feeling.

- Loveless -lacking love, feeling no love.
- Hurt- to feel or suffer bodily in pain or distress; to offend or grieve.
- Depressed -sad, gloomy.
- Crushed -a force that destroys or deforms.

- Bummed out -deciding that an experience is unpleasant or disappointing.

- Unhappy -miserable.

- Embarrassed -to be ashamed, self-conscious.

- Disappointed -discouraged by the failure of one's hopes.

- Devastated- to overwhelm with shock.

Sometimes people have been sad for so long, they think this is what life is supposed to feel like. It has become an ingrained pattern, the culture within their minds. Healing comes from knowing when to listen to your body and thoughts and discovering why your feelings are there. Decide you are through with that particular sorrow and write your script about your experience, your sadness, your fear, and what you have imagined. Write it down and then burn the page(s). Rewrite how you want to think about that part of your life and create your role as the person in charge, feeling courageous and successfully living through the horror as the person who wins, the champion. You can do it, Sheriff.

Joy

Your fourth finger gets a little taller when you feel joy. Happiness, contentment, laughter, gratitude, compassion for yourself and others, triumph, exhilaration, thrilled, ecstatic, blissful, cheerful, jolly – all of these describe the emotional place we typically want to spend most of our time. To get there, surround yourself with people who are happy, who support you in your dreams and encourage you. Feel the love with everyone and you will become and feel more loving. Allow other people to love you and you will love yourself more. Hang out with people who feel passion for life in whatever they are doing and you will feel more passionate, as well. Passion is contagious. Be enthusiastic about whatever it is you are doing and you will feel excited and motivated. Joy feels good. Practice living what brings you joy and you will have more of it. Love yourself enough to believe you are worthy of feeling joyful.

To be enthusiastic about living our lives is to be joyful, whether we are digging a hole in the backyard or making love with an extraordinary partner. We are joyful when we say to ourselves, 'This moment is bliss.' We are joyful when we stop being judgmental about what is "good" or "bad" but instead think, *I am being my greatest self right now. I am creating my legacy with every choice I make during every moment of my life.* Choose to be cheerful and you will be happy to live this life.

Some people think it is noble (courageous, moral) to feel miserable and have a belief system that is bleak (discouraging, depressing). If you or someone you know rolls this way, you are the only one who can change yourself. Feeling joy involves an ongoing responsibility to find delight and enthusiasm for this journey we are taking called life. Some people choose to sit around all day getting drunk and/or high and wonder why they still do not feel joy. It is because like everything else we build, it takes valuing the effort and focusing on the prize, the contentment that comes from enjoying what you are doing, fully awake and aware of thoughts and sensations during your experiences. In short, enjoy your life.

Make a list of everything you are grateful for and the tingle of joy will appear once again, possibly as soon as you write that first pleasurable thought that comes to your mind. If you are free and live in a country without war, that can be item number one on your list. Many people who share our planet are born into war-torn nations, poverty, or life-and-death circumstances. They need to work much harder to feel joy. Much harder.

If you are going to leave this moment and go into your mind, make it a joyful fantasy. If your thoughts are not increasing your levels of peace and happiness, take a deep breath, and bring yourself back here. Make it happen with the patient (understanding, calm, tolerant) practice.

Practice joy!

- Happy
- Jolly
- Radiant
- Good-natured
- Friendly
- Smiling
- Chipper
- Sociable
- Heart-warming
- Glee

- Bliss

- Ecstasy

- Light-hearted

- Festive

- Cheerful

- Welcoming

- Thrilled

- Delighted

- Elated

- On top of the world

You can raise your fourth finger and feel taller and stronger because you know you are brave enough to experience all of your feelings. If you are not pleased with how you feel, work to change your beliefs and practice thinking about what is healthier/better for you, and the new feeling will begin to manifest. It's just one more way to become the person you want to spend your life with.

*Pinky Finger = Your Relationships

Last but not least is your little finger, the one you used as a kid when you held out your hand looking into the eyes of a friend, and shouted, 'Pinky swear!' At the end of our lives, it is our relationships we must let go of as we slip out of this world, including the relationship we have had with ourselves. Whether it is with your lover, your best friend, your pet(s), your work, your higher power, hobbies, your favorite parts of life, you are in a relationship with everything. Look at your hand and smile at that little finger that hooks you in allegiance to a person, place or thing.

Our relationships help us create who we are, and so it is important to choose wisely. A large part of our identity is shaped by those people we trust to help us become who we want to be, and who tell us who we are. To have an authentic kinship with others requires us to be honest. That does not mean gush whatever you may be thinking and say it out loud, remember to use your filter. It means showing them who you are becoming and what it means to be you.

As Sheriff of Me Town, the wisest decision is to be real with your feelings when you are with those you trust. Otherwise, it is important to guard your heart, keeping your private thoughts and feelings close to your vest. You do not have to be dishonest. But remember, there is no law that says you must be "like an open book" at all times. Frankly, it is better much of the time to act as if you were preparing to win an academy award. Cheerful, friendly, interested, charming and intelligent is how you need to be perceived while at work or any gathering where you may not necessarily be completely comfortable. Your pleasantness will be admired as you guard your heart against people you do not want to let inside. Everyone wins and you, of course, look brilliant. Practice smiling in the mirror and get good at looking warm and friendly. This will pay off regardless of where you are, plus it feels great. You are charming your self.

Who do you want to be friends with, Melanie or Nikki Brie? Make your wisest choice, as always.

Melanie calls you once every six months and invites you to lunch, 'My treat!' The morning of your date (she told you she will be coming from somewhere else and will have to meet you there), she calls and cancels. 'It just never seems to work out! Maybe if you pick me up next time, I will be able to eat something planned. Gotta go!' Click.

In six months you go to her condo to pick her up for lunch. 'Just wait for me outside, my place is a mess.' You call to tell her you are there and she does not pick up her cell. You text her and she texts back, 'Coming!' Ten minutes later she runs to your car, jumps in, gives you a wet kiss on the cheek leaving lipstick behind, and announces, 'I don't have much time. Let's just go to this fast food place on the corner.' Once inside, you barely get a word in as she tells you all about her divorce and the cutie pie she met on a plane last month. You drop her off with your stomach feeling bloated and tense and she jumps out of the car yelling back at you, 'Sorry, I forgot my wallet today, Honey. Next time we will go someplace really nice!'

M = Melanie

E = Egotistical

T = Tiring

O = Offensive

W = Wicked

N = Nuisance

Nikki Brie calls you every six months and invites you to lunch, 'My treat!' The morning of your date she calls and confirms the 11:30 am time, 'Still good for you?' She picks you up in her clean car and goes to your door and knocks. 'You look beautiful! Are you ready? It is so great to see you – I can't wait to hear all about everything!' as she lightly holds your arm and leads you to where she parked the shiny car.

She takes you to lunch at the new café you read about in the paper last Sunday that got great reviews. She listens to your stories like they are the most interesting, exciting pieces of information she has ever heard. She laughs when you try to be funny and says, 'Oh friend, I have missed you!' She talks about her divorce for a bit, sharing, 'I know I need to trust the process and remember this is happening so I can be with someone who *really* loves me, not married to someone who acts as they would rather be somewhere else.' Tears well up in her eyes and she squeezes your hand, silently mouthing the words, 'Thank you,' because you have been listening intently to her without interruption. The check comes and Nikki Brie pays the bill and leaves a 25% tip. She drops you off and you promise each other to not wait so long until next time. Your heart feels full of love and your belly is pleasantly stuffed as you watch her drive away.

M = Mighty

E = Enormous

T = Thoughtful

O = Ownership

W = Winning

N = Noteworthy

Who will you choose? A vampire or an angel? The relationships you cultivate and value in Me Town are part of your legacy. Choose people who contribute to your power, not those who rob you of your light. Relationships give you what money cannot: A meaningful heart. You have a duty to yourself to protect it. Pinky swear!

CHAPTER 8

The Power Badge

The privilege of helping people discover how powerful they are has been one of the greatest rewards of my career. The Power Badge was created and developed to remind folks during counseling sessions and training workshops that they are completely fluid creatures, one of the many endowments of being able to live life as an interesting and resilient human being. I wanted to give people a prize, something to work and reward themselves with once they walked out of the room. The badge is yours because you have earned it, you have had the guts to look at yourself realistically and say,

'I can do better, and when I do, I will feel better. I have *that much* power. I do not have to park myself in someone's waiting room so they can "fix" me. I can get better using my own authority to run my life as I choose.'

I have given clients magic wands over the years that I happened to have on hand, but that wasn't sustainable. I used to say, 'Here is a magic wand. What do you want it to change for you?' They would laugh and we would get down to the business of how to change life for oneself, that yes life would be so much easier if we could have a magic wand. I needed a prize they could have for life, that would be easy to remember. The badge evolved, with me remembering my girlhood roots and how it made me feel when I would pretend I was the Sheriff and put my badge on. I did not have the words as a child, but it made me feel *empowered*, and I wanted to be able to help everyone feel as tough and confident as I did with my badge on. If I could do it, why couldn't everyone else if given a choice and a chance?

There have been so many clients I have seen who needed a power badge, but I had not thought of how to guide others to live life as the Sheriff of Me Town yet. When I was working as an intern in social work in my undergraduate years, I learned about giving a client something tangible they could hang onto, that had a lasting impact. I was assigned an extremely difficult case of an older man (let's call him Anthony) who was an alcoholic and immediately told me he had no intention of quitting alcohol once he was released from the program. Physically, he was in bad shape after the decades-long abuse of alcohol had ravaged his body. He was very likable with a great sense of humor and he sure told a good story. I was having a hard time accepting the fact that once he walked out the door he would not last long.

One day when we were talking about his life, I asked him if he could make something about his life history completely different, what would that be. I was floored when he told me, this ex-marine and professional mechanic for many years, father of six children, that what he would have made different was having the motivation to learn how to read! Anthony was so clever, he told me all of the ways he figured out how to "pass" as a reader. I could hardly believe how smart he was, so imaginative and what a great actor to have pulled this secret off for so many years and in so many different settings.

I asked him, 'Would you like me to teach you how to read?'

Tears came and he said, 'I'm not smart enough.'

I smiled broadly and said, 'You are one of the smartest people I have ever met. You not only know how to sign your name and write basic words, but you also have a gift of gab, and that along with your creative, intelligent brain, you have accomplished so much. We've got nothing but time. Let me help you with this, you can do it.'

He agreed, and I proceeded to bring in the alphabet flashcards, and we began this magnificent journey together. I was smart enough myself to know not to mention this to my on-site supervisor who would have brought this endeavor to a screeching halt. I wanted to help Anthony, and this was a project he was willing to take on. Over the three months, I was with him, I would sit down every session and do a check-in to see how he was coping, and give me the opportunity to help him reframe some thoughts he was having that were not working to his advantage. Then I would take out my backpack and lay the teaching materials on the desk, and we would begin again.

He learned quickly, and by the time my internship was over he was reading at the 4th grade level. At our last session, I handed him a gift that was wrapped in tissue and a big bow. He was delighted when he opened the book by Dr. Seuss, "Green Eggs and Ham!" I had inscribed a personal message to him in the front cover, reminding him he is smart enough to move mountains and accomplish whatever he put his mind to. I told him he was a joy and I would never forget him. He looked up and said to me, 'I'll never forget you either, Julia.' He opened the book, and page by page, he read it to me, all 769 words with the happiest smile on his face I had ever seen. It was the first time I cried with a client but certainly not the last. He had his book, he had a new identity, he had proof he was intelligent. I did not know it at the time, but I had given him his Power Badge.

If we choose to **remember**, we have the capability and competence to ignite our driving force to become both formidable and commanding of our selves. When feeling exhausted from grief or pain, when we are in our weakest moments, it is imperative we have a symbol that reminds us we have the authority to implement our opportunities, to remember we are a life force that is evolving, moment by moment, day by day, and year by year. We are not placed in granite, a deceased symbol in Mount Rushmore. We are far from extinct, more accurately we are a living treasure that with every beat of our hearts we are teeming with new circumstances and possibilities to reinvent ourselves. We are not obsolete but alive and kicking, animated and full of life as long as we have breath. To be disorganized and forgetful of the variety of strengths one has, may lead to believing you are inadequate, a watered-down version of what was once your best self. The Power Badge is a symbol that represents all the ways you can remember you are significant and strong. What you create and develop in the different categories of your badge is your masterpiece, the work of art that is you.

The badge is placed over your heart so you never forget to remember you are an active creature with some 37.2 trillion cells all working very hard on your behalf because they belong to you. You are transforming, adapting, progressing and revising yourself with every challenge that comes your way. You are not glued to the past, although sometimes it might seem that way. No, the Power Badge does not allow for believing you have been beaten. You may lose a fight, but you will continue your crusade with purpose and direction. You will remember this because you march with your head up and your chest out in Me Town, and to forget is the hiccup that abandons your greatest ally, the person you have the most in common with, yourself. There is nothing more important than taking care of yourself. Without self-care, you will have little to give.

I have worked with literally thousands of people, helping them to figure out a way to remember "Anything is possible because I am still here." How to remember we are our greatest self, was what I learned from watching the movie, "The Wizard of Oz" as a child. Every spring it was televised and became a tradition in my life to watch it with my family. My grandparents would be out of town making their yearly trek to Florida for a warm vacation, and my siblings and I would be at their house watching the show because they had a color television, and we did not, ours was black and white. Part of the magic of that movie, produced in 1939 when most movies were made in black and white, was when Dorothy landed in OZ after being swept away and taken there by a tornado. She landed with a hard thump, and when she opened the door of her house to look outside, everything was in **color** for the rest of the movie! My grandmother told me when she watched it in the theater, as Dorothy opened the door everyone in the movie theater let out a dramatic 'Ohhhhh!' of disbelief. I loved that movie, and I learned that the human qualities of courage, learning and love for others and yourself could not be given to you, you had to learn how to do this for yourself.

My favorite part of the movie was at the end when the Cowardly Lion, the Scarecrow, the Tinman and Dorothy with her little dog, Toto all survived the Wicked Witch and her nasty monkeys and evil spells, by sticking together and helping each other along the way. What they asked the Wizard at the end of the movie was to give them what they wanted most, what they did not realize they already had. What he gave them was a symbol (a Power Badge), something to remind them of how much strength they did have. For the Cowardly Lion, it was a medal of bravery he could wear around his neck that said "courage" on it. Once he had that medal around his neck, he realized he was not only daring but had true grit. The scarecrow did not realize he had a brain because he had nothing to prove it, after all, his head was made of straw. But he had been coming up with different strategies throughout the entire movie to get them out of trouble and figure out what to do. The Wizard of Oz presented Scarecrow with a diploma, a THD, a "Doctor of Thinkology," (his Power Badge), and that reminder was all it took for him to speak out an equation that even startled him that he knew it. The Tinman did not remember all of the times he started to cry and almost rusted himself with his tears. He needed a reminder that indeed he did have a heart and he had been showing and feeling the love during the entire adventure. The Wizard gave him a testimonial and presented him with a ticking red clock in the shape of a heart (his power badge). The Wizard reminded him,

'Remember, a heart is not judged by how much you love, but how much you are loved by others.'

Finally, Dorothy, who wanted to go home where she was safe and life was predictable again, was told by Glenda, the Good Witch in Oz, she always had the power to go home, to Kansas. 'You had to learn it for yourself.'

Dorothy realized if her heart's desire (her Power Badge) cannot be found in her own backyard, she never really lost it to begin with.

The Wizard of Oz is a fabulous movie filled to the brim with wisdom and lessons, if you have not watched it lately or have never seen it before, make it your movie night this weekend. It is brilliant and a ton of fun. It helped shape a future counselor into realizing everybody needs a badge, some sort of reminder of who is in charge and of who you are becoming, one choice at a time.

In Me Town, you have all the power. Start right now by saying to yourself, 'I am Sheriff of Me Town and I have all the power here.' Repeat this to yourself frequently throughout each day. When you do, your life – and town – will become the one you want to run. You will create habitual thinking and nail down the belief you own a Power Badge, even when you sleep and how you behave in your dreams. You will make changes and keep changing with the confidence that comes with being an official, responsible for the outcomes that describe your life. It will become a comfortable, natural place to go when you need to bolster your confidence. Make it a habit to touch your chest over your heart. You can do this.

How to Measure Your Strength

Living your life using all the power you can muster during each moment leads you to triumph. Your Power Badge is your mark on this world; it is the emblem you wear in your mind to guide and empower yourself. It is an honor to wear it, because having it on means you are alive, you are always in charge of who you are and you have the opportunity to develop, grow, and practice your strength. Make this a habit by picturing your badge over your heart as you go about your day, Sheriff, and remember it is always there.

The quality of your mental, physical, spiritual, social, sexual, and emotional strength will wax and wane as the result of your choices and current conditions. That being said, you have the control to develop your toughness, as measured by the intensity of your focus and your willingness to be tested. Your Power Badge and how you wear it is your distinctive feature that, over time, becomes your reputation. You portray who you are to yourself and the world with this symbol by knowing how to strengthen from within and remember to forgive yourself when you do not feel strong. Develop your confidence with your badge and the attitude: "Show me what you've got life. I'm ready."

Your Power Badge is your best reminder that life is not about solving one problem after another, but an adventure to be lived with gusto and passion. Live your adventures, do not label what happens as problems but as opportunities to grow stronger. Let your Power Badge guide your way along the journey that distinguishes you and makes you one of a kind.

To assist in being consistently honest with yourself, I have developed an ongoing assessment for gauging how strong you are at any particular juncture. Remember that change is a verb and we are always transforming and altering ourselves into this beautiful being that we are becoming. At times we all look back on our lives and think, *I could have done better*. Be grateful for this hindsight, for reflecting on past mistakes will grow wisdom. Do not judge, but learn and let this insight motivate your discipline, training your thoughts and behavior so you can improve as best you can.

Before we take a look at this assessment for measuring your performance, make this pledge and say it out loud,

'I, (say your name), formally promise myself and the citizens of the world, to do my best at growing my personal power. I will live my life fulfilling my obligation to myself and the rest of humanity to leave this planet a better, stronger place than how I found it when I arrived. This is my Power Badge pledge.'

MEASURE YOUR STRENGTH

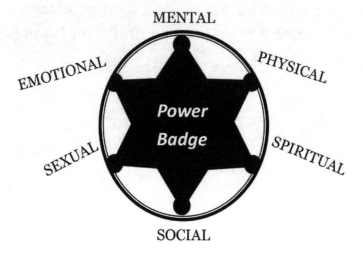

CHAPTER 9

Measuring Your Mental Strength

We become what we think. If you believe that whatever happens throughout life is useful for growing strength and wisdom, then you will not judge what happens to you, but accept it. It may be difficult for you to think about an unexpected betrayal, for instance, but you can do so by making focused decisions, rather than living in a state of confusion and worry.

Mental strength gets top billing because it is the only part of our lives we have control over. So how do we become stronger mentally? How do we assess our progress? Whether your IQ is 65 or 160, you need to perform push-ups for your brain.

How? By solving problems, taking risks, and practicing how to learn about what you don't know. Reaching out for more knowledge, and in this age of YouTube, you can learn how to do anything. As long as you have a phone you have your personal library, teachers, and training ground for everything you are interested in. Go to edx.org and browse the 2,500 courses you can take online for free, and look for other free resources. Your local library is a seeker's paradise, it is like playing Candyland for your mind. The world is your oyster, and your discoveries will be the pearls that you find in the countless learning opportunities you have right now, at this moment.

When I attended college it was not because I wanted to study and become stronger mentally. I enrolled because my plan to escape college by joining the Coast Guard failed. I had a recruiter and every intention of sailing away and never going to school again. This ultimately failed because I did not lose the 30 pounds to qualify for the Guard. I also came up with a plan to go to California and become a rock star. I was writing songs like crazy and I loved to sing and perform. I was in chorus and choir, I had roles in high school musicals, variety shows and plays, and after all, I was voted most talented in my class senior year. This idea failed because I did not own a car and had $300 in the bank. My choices were to either go to college (away from home) or go to work and get an apartment. Since my focus on learning up to that point had mostly been about socializing and having a daily party in my life, I was less than thrilled. I chose to leave the house and attend school because after being accepted into the University of Missouri – Columbia, it was a good school and a great place to have fun – that was the word on the street. Fast forward four years and a bachelor's degree in social work, with a GPA of less than 3.0. I could not find a job in social work partly because it was a time in our nation's history when President Carter was in office and the economy experienced high inflation and slow economic growth. Despite our president's best efforts, we had an energy crisis and a recession in 1980. Professionals with master's degrees in social work were being laid off and were not finding work, so I searched for employment that would afford me opportunities to work with people in need of help.

I landed a job working with profoundly disabled individuals who lived at a large institution, and they helped me grow up. I learned many lessons there, and the residents taught me taking gifts like sight, hearing, walking, talking, eating, bathing, and the ability to analyze complicated problems and challenges for granted, was a big mistake. They taught me true courage and showed me what tenacity and not giving up really looked like. They sparked my desire to use my brain to make the world a better place, I now had no excuse. During that time I applied to graduate school for counseling psychology and was rejected because my GPA was too low, I didn't qualify. I knew that if I wanted to counsel people, I needed a master's degree, that was a no brainer. I knew I had to keep trying so I made an appointment with the dean of the College of Education to make my case as to why he should admit me. I was willing to plead, grovel, and do whatever it took to get in. I walked into that appointment and was asked to take a seat. I knew immediately by his body language and vocal tone the person in front of me was not at all interested in my presence and was prepared to reiterate the rejection letter I received. He was simply going through the motions of my appeal. I stared at his decorated wall of diplomas and certificates as he shuffled through papers in my file.

'You simply do not have the academic achievement we expect from our graduate students. I'm sorry,' he quickly responded.

I took a deep pause and my persuasion skills that were a part of my personality perked up inside me. Little did I know at the time that the only A+ I would ever make in my life was in my Persuasion Skills course while studying for my doctorate ten years later. My persuasive personality would serve me well later, as a professional counselor and trainer. At that moment I needed the guts to say out loud what I was thinking.

'To tell you the truth, *Dr. So and So,* I did not realize I seriously wanted to learn until I had this job working with people who showed me what struggle *really* looks like...' and I proceeded to tell him my story. I convinced him I was worthy by using my mental strength and using my words, summoning my bravery looking him directly in his eyes, and approaching this meeting as the most important performance and show of my life. I performed well. After respecting me enough to listen to my humbled insight and realization I needed the institution to help me get to where I wanted to go, he put on his glasses and said,

'Okay, I'll tell you what I will do. I will let you take one semester of classes, 15 hours, as an undeclared major. You get a 4.0 (straight A's), and I'll let you in.'

I have no doubt he was simply getting more money for the university and did not believe I could accomplish this, but that didn't matter. I stood up, shook his hand, and thanked him for the opportunity. I spoke with his assistant about how to systematically enroll in classes, knowing I had never made straight A's in my life. 'Let me show you what I can do,' I said silently to both him and myself. I quit my job and turned my full-time occupation into going to every class, every day, a first for me as I had worked part-time throughout my bachelor's degree. I read the books and materials, enthusiastically engaging with the other students and professors, studying for quizzes and exams, turning in all of my papers and assignments, and getting enough sleep. When I had finished my exams and the semester was over, I made an appointment to revisit the dean in mid-December. I walked towards his desk, laid my grade report in front of him, and said, 'Am I in?' Every class had an 'A' sitting right beside it. It was one of those profound moments in life one never forgets.

He picked up the grades and shook his head back and forth, looked up at me, and said, 'Welcome to this college. Keep up the good work.' I did keep up the good work and learned to love learning. I graduated with my master's degree in counseling psychology and wrote my thesis about a unique group I had organized of students who were seeking personal growth and transformation. I facilitated the group as the only counselor and conducted a qualitative analysis of their experiences based upon their self-reports. I challenged my mental strength and I prevailed. If I can do it, you can do it. Go forth and conquer your mental strength, starting with this assessment.

On a scale from 1 to 10, think about how often you are willing to do each of the following:

1. Do you actively monitor whether you are merely acting out of patterns and habits in your outlook of what is going on, or do you seek new views in your mental world, remembering to look around? Do you ask, 'What is different about my truth by paying attention in this manner? Do I need to take a deep breath and just be open to a new reality?'

2. Are you practicing good judgment by looking at life with focus, or are you determining many solutions at one time? Is a particular thought important or trivial? Does every thought have the potential for incredible change, or are you stuck in the deception that if you don't change you will be safe and sound?

3. Do you see events as good or bad, or do you see the potential in whatever is going on, or has happened, without judgment? What initially may seem catastrophic may open the door for something so extraordinary it cannot even be imagined.

4. How many books have you read in the last six months? When was the last time you went to the library? How often do you study to learn something new? Do you play games, do crossword puzzles, learn songs, play a musical instrument,

listen to different kinds of music, look at or engage in art or analyze life from different perspectives?

5. How often do you engage in stimulating conversations with other people, opening your mind to new paradigms, new ways of thinking about life, yourself, other people, and the rest of the world? Do you travel outside your daily routine by taking trips (even day trips), walks, go to the movies, concerts, or the theater? Do you let yourself just "be" and not define yourself by your relationships, job, where you live, how much money you have, or your past?

6. How often do you meditate and listen to the thoughts in your mind? Do you know what you are thinking about? Are you listening? What are the stories playing over and over? Do you need to alter or reject these stories? Do you feel addicted to thinking about certain people, places, or things?

7. Are you taking time to discover how you could be in each moment, or are you just reacting to someone or something automatically like you usually do?

8. Do you let your mind rest and relax, or are you always "on"? How easy is it for you to laugh and find humor throughout your day?

9. Do you tell yourself a story about your life that is uplifting, nurturing, forgiving, encouraging, and loving? Or do you tell yourself a story about your life that is critical, judgmental, full of self-doubt, negative, and pessimistic? Your brain will believe whatever you tell it, so make your story the one you want to live with. Each moment you have the opportunity to edit, refine, and change who you are as a result of a new narrative of what you believe reality is right now. If you don't like it, change your belief system. Allow yourself to be fluid in your thoughts rather than rigid in thinking.

10. How often do you ask yourself for help in the morning, and then tell yourself, 'Well done!' at bedtime? Appreciating your mind by acknowledging it and nurturing your mental strength involves reinforcing the desire to grow your mental power with purpose. Do you value becoming smarter? Do you say to yourself, 'Stay strong,' during stressful and difficult times? Do you want the courage to change who you are by practicing being different?

Mental Strength Assessment

Now, look at your Power Badge and assign a number between 1 and 10 as your mental strength. Number 1 would go something like this, 'Wow, I am not paying attention to my mind at all. I'm in a rut and need to get busy. I am boring myself. I have an addiction to thinking.' Number 5 might be, 'Hey, I've been paying attention to nurturing my mental qualities, but there is a lot more I can do!' Number 10 might say, 'I do believe I qualify as a mental giant!' You get the idea.

Use any number you like that seems to be the most accurate for you today, knowing that this number can, and will change over time. Your mental strength is powerful as long as you are paying attention to it.

Now after reviewing your assessment you may notice you need to improve in some areas. Don't be so hard on yourself but understand there is an opportunity for you to grow in this area. Below are some things you can do to help you increase your mental strength. Try one or all of them, until you find the best for you. You can do it, Sheriff!

Journaling. Write down your thoughts once a day and analyze how you think about anything that interests you. Let your ideas flow out of you and write for as long as it amuses you, whether that's a paragraph or three pages. Notice how organized or unorganized your thoughts seem to be, and then rewrite some of your sentences so that they make more sense, are clearer and more to the point. Remember to include who, what, where, when and why as part of your story, like a good journalism student would do. If your journal is lacking humor add a joke or funny story. If you find your words lack depth or meaning, rewrite so it is more interesting. Practicing your narrative in this way will help your thinking become more organized and interesting. It will also help you appreciate how unique your voice is and validate for you that you have some very cool things to say and share.

Play a Game of Debate With a Friend or Family Member. Make the topic something simple, and once you have more confidence using your voice and words to express your opinion, then the next game can be more complicated and so on. For example, 'What is your favorite movie and why?' Express your view and then listen to hers/his. Now discuss who made the best points and who was most persuasive and why. You may declare a winner or call it a tie. The goal of this game is to improve how you express your mental strength, develop and build it by becoming more confident through *practice.*

The Dictionary Game. I invented this many years ago at a party and have been playing it ever since. It is possible other people invented and play it, too, I certainly hope so because it is a lot of fun. You will need at least two people to play. Here are the rules. Someone in the group holds the dictionary so no one can see it. S/he finds a common word, such as brain, and reads the definition out loud without saying the word. The first person to guess the word and say it out loud wins that round. Start with simple words, although these can be surprisingly deceptive. To change it up, after ten words are played with, trade places and have someone else take control of this tell-all book. Now, s/he reads a word out loud and you have to describe the definition. What does this word mean? Give people credit if they come close. If they are completely wrong, then it becomes a "close but no cigar" type of situation and time to read another word, waiting for the most accurate definition to call it a win. Words are your friends, Sheriff, get more acquainted with them.

Reading For Fun and Challenge. Check out some easy magazines to look throughout for pure enjoyment, then graduate yourself to National Geographic and read it cover to cover. Not only will you be introduced to some words you have never seen before, but you will also have some interesting stories to share during dinner. If you want to test your brain, check out Scientific American magazine and see if it looks like English or gibberish. Either way, you will be doing one-legged push-ups for your mind. Conduct this same exercise only with books. Pick a very easy to read one and go through it quickly. Then read another just for fun book and you can move on to something a bit more challenging, maybe a murder mystery you can figure out as you flip through the pages. The more you read the faster at reading you will become, and your focus and feeling "sharp" will improve.

Brain Teasers. Words searches, crossword puzzles, sudoku, any type of brain teaser will strengthen you mentally. Read opinions and editorials and see if you agree with the writer, and why. Do you feel yourself becoming stronger already in the smarts department?

Learn How to Find Rest With Yourself Mentally. Every mind deserves a bit of peace and quiet, and this requires focused intent. Learn basic meditation skills so your mental life can rest a bit. We can get a bit noisy between our ears sometimes, and a little mental vacation can bring peace and calm, another necessary skill for mental strength. Start by finding a quiet comfortable place, and pay attention to your breath. Easy does it, go ahead and slow it down paying attention to the warmth of the air, the sensation of your lungs becoming fuller and then emptying. How is your body temperature? If you are chilly get a blanket, if you are warm turn on a fan or take some clothing off. Pay attention to your body and it will help you take a vacation from your mind. Do some isometric and relaxation exercises starting with your toes and working your way up to ankles, calves, buttocks, arms, hands, shoulders, neck, the muscles in your face. Smile, frown, blow out air, and move your lips all around, raise and lower your eyebrows, make your nostrils flare and relax. Whatever comes into your mind, look at it without judgement and let it go. Do this 15 minutes a day and you will strengthen your mind by giving it a much-needed recess.

CHAPTER 10

Measuring Your Physical Strength

The stronger you are physically, the stronger you are in every category of your Power Badge. The Power Badge is your mark on this world, which includes measuring your capacity and potential for physical strength. To test your physical strength, start by taking a deep breath. Inhale peace, exhale love. Tighten the muscles in your biceps, and now relax them. Do the same with your calves, point your toes, tighten your thighs and buttocks, move your head around your neck, slowly relaxing your shoulder muscles. Bring those shoulders up to your ears, and then relax.

Next, contort your face; smile, frown, move your eyebrows up and down, move your muscles around your cheekbones, ears, and jaw, use all those places on your face you count on to make your facial expressions convey what you want and who you are. Welcome to your body. Welcome home.

My late, great friend, Annette was a fitness expert who was completely non-judgmental when it came to advising her clients about developing their physical strength. It did not matter to her if you could run ten feet or ten miles, she just encouraged you to enjoy it and celebrate the fact that you were interested in getting stronger. I, along with hundreds of other people, will miss her kindness, generosity, and positive attitude until the day we die. No matter how much I was struggling with a particular exercise or workout, she would always call me, "champ" and tell me I looked really good. It was because of her encouragement that I lifted weights and developed my body where I hardly recognize myself in the mirror. Thank you, Annette, for helping me respect my body's potential for strength and being one of the best friends I have ever had. I miss you every day and will always carry you in my heart.

I got a varsity letter in swimming in high school, butterfly was my stroke. It was the first year the high school had opened the opportunity to girls, and although we inherited the boys hand me down sweats while they received brand new ones, I didn't mind it. I was just grateful for the new law prohibiting discrimination because we were female, and the opportunity to swim again. I was on a local team as a kid and this challenge helped me build my confidence, even though I was not very fast. I swam butterfly in the individual 200 (four times back and forth in the pool) because nobody else on the girl's high school team knew the stroke and were not as fast as me. I still had room for improvement, and I was not very good at butterfly either. In fact, in our first meet, I almost didn't finish. I couldn't breathe and wanted to stop swimming. I remember my coach and the rest of the team standing at the end of my lane and screaming, 'Don't stop! Keep going! You can do it! Keep going!' Coming in last was better than not coming in at all.

Over time, I improved, and my best memory of being on the team was when we were competing against another high school in a district with wealthy students. I stepped up on the block as the only member of my team representing us, and looked at the three swimmers I would be competing against. *Oh, there was no way I will place against any of them,* I thought to myself. They looked like they had personal trainers at the age of seventeen. They were all huge, with muscles showing in places I didn't even know I had muscles. Yes, I was completely intimidated and felt sick to my stomach. Then I looked over at my team and my coach, cheering me on as usual. I could read the looks on their faces, and I could tell they were acting as if I *actually* had a chance to place. I thought if they believed I could beat one of those girls, then so could I. Plus, it was our last meet at the end of the season, my last opportunity to shape our team and create the mindset of winners. 'Swimmers, take your marks!' the official shouted before firing the blank. I hit the water with an incredible dive and heard the whistles screaming to stop. One of the opposing team members had a false start, she had left the block above the water before the official start, and we all had to get out of the water and start again. Now I was *really* feeling so nervous my legs were shaking and my breathing was very rapid. 'Shake it off, shake it off!' my coach was yelling at me. I shook my arms and legs and thought just swim as fast as you possibly can, swim fast! No more false starts and we were all in the water. After my first flip turn, I looked over and saw I was not last but ahead of one of them! I felt a rush of adrenaline and kicked my dolphin feet more powerfully than I ever had before in my life. Down to the blocks, flip turn, two more lengths to go. This time when I was at the opposite end with one lane to go, there was only one swimmer ahead of me. That was it, I don't remember breathing after that moment. I tagged the wall at the finish, looked over, and I saw two of them swimming into the wall. I came in second! It was my greatest athletic achievement in my life up to that point, and the natural high I felt cannot be described. I got out of the pool to my crazy team and coach jumping up and down, hugging me, and congratulating me. It didn't matter to them I wasn't in the first place, I was celebrated as a hero, and I felt like one. It was in college during my fencing class that I had that same feeling, the same high, when I beat every man in my class during an epic practice I will never forget.

The benefits of physical exercise are plentiful and include so much more than becoming physically stronger, as can be seen in my examples of when I felt absolute triumph. The benefits of regular exercise and physical activity can be achieved by anyone, regardless of age or physical ability. Exercise helps you control your weight because you are burning calories. You can figure out how to add more exercise to your day by lifting cans of soup in your wheelchair, or parking farther away to get more steps in, taking the stairs instead of the elevator, and throwing yourself into your household chores and outside cleanup duties. Exercise also combats health conditions and diseases like high blood pressure, heart disease, and it even helps combat high cholesterol by decreasing unhealthy triglycerides and boosts your good cholesterol (HDL), which helps your blood flow more smoothly. Exercise can help lift depression and lower anxiety, helps prevent falls, and improve cognitive function. It will boost your energy levels, promotes better sleep, and can put the spark back in your sex life, increasing your confidence and improving your appearance. I believe exercise is the fountain of youth, and when I am feeling unmotivated or just plain tired, I remind myself of this and that the process can not only be enjoyable, but I feel so much more relaxed and stronger when I am done. Exercise is an important tool to build your strength and make sure heaven forbid, you have the strength to defend yourself, lift yourself, and even save yourself in an emergency.

The Power Badge strengths are connected and influence one another all the time. Stay focused on your body, it is your permanent home, for life. Take good care of it with good nutrition, take your vitamins, make sure you drink plenty of water which is more liquid than you think it is. Take care of your digestion and bowel habits. Don't abuse alcohol and drugs which can be risky to physical strength, so use with common sense and more than an ounce of caution. Make an appointment for your yearly physical exam and visit the health care team if you are having any concerns. Get plenty of rest and sleep and do not believe you are being lazy when you do. Taking the time to rejuvenate yourself with rest, is just as important as active movement.

Own your body with confidence as the Sheriff of Me Town. Walk tall with your chest sticking out, and if you are in a wheelchair or differently-abled, remember to lift yourself as best as you can, envisioning yourself on the ground as you own it. Use your physical power to reflect the confidence that comes with taking care of your body, being aware of what it is doing and how it feels. Practice being "body awake," let your physical strength take charge when you need to protect, express, and enjoy yourself physically.

Now, let's measure your physical strength and how well you are paying attention to your anatomy. Remember, you are your physical guard wherever you are. Whether you can do 25 push-ups or none, you need to travel through life treating your body with respect. If you feel weak, start small and don't overdo it or you can get hurt. If walking around the block is as far as you can go, that is okay. Next time you will plan to go a little farther. If you can only pick up a five-pound weight, that's okay, work with that amount and increase your repetitions. Then go up to ten pounds, or increase your push-ups by one, your sit-ups by two. The point is that you are moving and striving to build endurance, stamina, and physical power.

On a scale of 1 to 10, think about how well you take care of your body in the following aspects:

1. Use your voice. When you use your voice, you are showing your strength through how you sound. Use your diaphragm muscle and make sure you have plenty of air in your lungs so when you speak, you can convey and have a vocal tone that communicates confidence. Use eye contact, stand tall and use other nonverbal physical communication. Speak with enough volume so people cannot only hear you, they translate your message as coming from someone with the confidence that accompanies a person in authority, which you are, Sheriff. Stand up with your chest out and say out loud with strength and pride, 'I have all the power,' and mean it. Because you do have all the power, all the time. No one has the power to be you, except you.

How do you sound when you are communicating with others? How do you sound to yourself? Is your voice strong and controlled, or shaky and weak? Are you willing to use your voice as a way of protecting and defending yourself when you are being threatened, or in the presence of a predator? When you make a verbal statement of fact, do not say it as if it were a question, with your voice getting higher at the end of the sentence. It is not a question, so use your vocal inflection to make your statement a clear and resounding message. When you make it sound like a question and raise your voice higher at the end of the message, you sound unsure of yourself and lacking confidence. This is a habit you need to break if this is you. Practice using your voice when you are at home, preferably in front of a mirror so you can see what you look like. Talk to yourself on the recording device on your phone and make changes to your vocal style if you want to. Do you look like the Sheriff in the mirror that you are, or are your shoulders slumped and bent over, looking more like a person who has been defeated? Practice saying these words with a strong voice, projecting volume and confidence: 'Back up, you are standing too close to me. Stop talking, I need to be able to speak also. I am not afraid of you.' Use different experiences you have had and relive them using your powerful voice. It's been there all along. Hold your body still with all of your strength and courage and communicate nonverbally that you are not afraid by showing eye contact and a solid positioning of your chest and shoulders.

2. Are you exercising most days at least 30 minutes each day, as recommended by the American Heart Association? When you feel stiff in your back do you stretch as soon as possible? Do you stretch throughout the day? Do you make exercise fun (e.g. a brisk walk at lunchtime to enjoy some fresh air and sunshine), or does it feel like punishment (60 minutes on the treadmill, no matter what)? Do you lift weights, do push-ups, sit-ups, play sports, or ping pong? Have you practiced yoga, or what about Zumba? Any activity that gets you moving and enjoying yourself is good exercise. Whether it is fun or drudgery will decide how often you move intentionally with a focus on developing your strength and stamina.

3. What are you putting in your mouth to fuel your body? Hard-boiled eggs or donuts? Do you commit most of the time to make healthy choices, like eating a minimum of five

servings of fruits and vegetables every day as recommended by the American Cancer Society? Do you mostly drink water or sugary drinks? When it comes to alcohol, do you drink in moderation, or do you often overdo it? Are you a smoker? If so, do you smoke a pack of cigarettes a day or perhaps just one occasionally while enjoying a cocktail? Indulging, like having a big, juicy steak, loaded baked potato, chopped salad, and wine for dinner (and don't forget a piece of pie for dessert) occasionally is not going to kill you. Life is to be enjoyed. Eat and drink slowly, enjoying each flavor and texture. Certainly, we cannot eat a big dinner like that every night, but we are allowed to treat ourselves and enjoy indulgence responsibly. Cheers!

4. Since we live in a nation of insomniacs, I must ask, how much sleep are you getting? (Seven to eight hours is recommended). Do you keep your phone out of your bedroom at night? Do you wash your sheets and blankets and keep a clean, cool room that you enjoy being in? Do you make sure you are not guzzling fluids before bedtime so you don't wake up in the night and have to trot to the bathroom? Did you know that your muscles grow at night when you are sleeping? How's that for an incentive for valuing sleep as the way of recharging your batteries so you can become stronger?

5. How often do you physically touch your body, massage yourself, and assess what you may need to be paying more attention to? Do you urinate at least once every three hours

(except at night)? Are you on friendly terms with your bowels? Do you use eye drops? Lip balm? Lotion? Are you taking your medication(s) as prescribed? Are you keeping your doctor appointments, and are you prepared with concerns and questions to communicate effectively and efficiently with the physician?

6. Every six months you need to go to the dentist and have your teeth cleaned and maintained. If you have to force yourself to go, then do it. A strong body requires good dental hygiene. Are you brushing at least twice a day? Flossing daily?

7. If you are having a good time, tell that to your face. If you are not having a good time, tell your face to act in accordance with whatever is to your advantage at that moment. There is no rule that says your face must accurately reflect what is really going on. Use your face as a cherished component of physical strength; having control over what your face is doing is as important as having good balance and strong muscles. If you need to have a blank expression to gain composure, then put that face on. If you need to hide fear or anger based upon the circumstances, a smile might be just the ticket to have the power during the exchange. If you feel like crying and it is neither the time nor place for this intense expression of emotion, you may want to look away and focus your eyes on an object to cover up what your face feels like doing. There is no rule that says you have to be genuine every second. Give yourself permission to be an actor worthy of an academy

award-winning performance if this is to your advantage at the moment.

8. Are you working on good balance exercises? Do you know how to do planks to build your core? Abdominal exercises can mean the difference between tripping over a rock and falling or catching yourself and preventing breaking your wrist or hip. Do you know how to fall into a roll? Have you practiced?

9. Do you keep yourself warm and dry? Do you just soldier on and not pay attention to that rock in your shoe? How body-aware are you at every interval throughout your day? Taking good care of Me Town means constant surveillance and paying attention to the landscape that is your physical strength and stamina. Are you overweight? Underweight? Do you weigh yourself regularly? Do you know your blood pressure, cholesterol, body mass index (BMI), and heart rate? Just like performing regular maintenance on your vehicle, if you maintain your body, it will be more reliable and need fewer repairs.

10. Can you take a punch? Do you know basic self-defense skills? If you need to run from danger, can you run? Do you take in your surroundings and prepare for the possibility that you could be in danger in an instant, whether from an accident, animal, person, a bulge in the sidewalk, lightning heat, or cold? Being physically strong requires valuing and respecting

your body as much as remembering to pay attention to it. Are you paying attention?

Physical Strength Assessment

Now feel yourself from head to toe and decide what number you are going to assign to the physical strength of your power badge. Are you a 1, 'I got out of bed this morning and was so stiff I could hardly make it to the bathroom while I was choking for water. I feel so dehydrated.' Or a 5, 'Well, I have been taking pretty good care of myself physically, but I do hope I can get my pants zipped up this morning.' Or a 10, 'I have never felt better or stronger in my whole life and I just turned 75.' You are physically strong as long as you are paying attention and caring for your body.

CHAPTER 11

Measuring Your Spiritual Strength

"**O**ne Truth, Many Paths" was the name of a radio program I used to listen to in college. It changed my spiritual life because it taught me that what happens to me becomes my truth and my direction. I realized the spiritual road I choose to take, belongs to me. As children, we are led by our parents and caregivers to create our spiritual beliefs based upon what they believe. That may be attending a church, mosque, temple, tribal sacred ceremonies, or taking regular hikes in the woods in silence, paying attention to the beauty that surrounds us in nature. Your spiritual life is as unique to you as is every other element in your Power Badge, it belongs to you and you have all the power to shape, design and practice it as you wish.

Building your spiritual strength is as easy as accepting yourself as a sacred one-of-a-kind energy who has been given the opportunity to live, to love and to ultimately depart this world by leaving your own distinct mark of who and how you behaved when you were here. Some people work on growing spirituality by attending an organized faith community. Others feel empowered by living as an atheist; a nonbeliever of organized religion. That being said, I have known atheists who to me, felt like the most spiritual people I have ever known because their capacity to love and nurture was enormous. Just being in their presence felt like I was being given the gifts of compassion, attention, joy, and an open heart for me and my existence. When I am with someone who seems to be a spiritual person, it feels like I matter to them when I am with them, I count as worthy and important. For others, the connection may be a spiritual experience because the person is so well versed in holy text and scripture, they are experts in one religion or even many. Spiritual strength is important because for all of us, sometimes the healthiest choice we can make is to believe in something or someone we cannot see but have the belief that that entity or that person is here. This can give us the faith and hope we are not alone in this infinite universe, and that something or someone will come along and help us, that we are never alone. To rely on your spirit, Sheriff, is to believe that there is someone or something that is going to help you and exists beside or within you. Hold on and the spirit that is known or unknown, will appear. That is called having faith, and faith is free and available to all of us who are willing to be optimistic. It is the conviction of hanging on despite the odds. Faith will fortify you with the confidence that you will prevail through every test of your strength that will be thrown your way. Since there will be many more tests than we would have personally requested, it is the greatest skill to build as a part of your spiritual life. Hold on for one more day, you are never alone in spirit, Sheriff. Practice having faith.

Who you are on the inside, your inner being that is holy simply because you exist, is where your spiritual strength is born. Following your instincts and living your life with all of your heart is the part of you that can be felt with such intensity, it is sometimes difficult to describe. Spiritual strength is knowing deep in the core of who you have become, that you have had experiences, but those experiences do not have you. You are bigger than what has happened. You are stronger than a memory. We have all suffered from horrible experiences in our lives, and spiritual strength helps us during those difficult times. Deciding we're not going to ignore this trauma because that doesn't work and it keeps coming back to haunt us, nor remain devastated by it – engulfed by worry and sorrow, involves cultivating our spiritual strength to help us grow from the experience and become better people.

For some, this journey includes having faith in a higher power. It involves trusting the process of life and accepting what is beyond our control. We know we can transform darkness into light when we use tools we have on hand and live with an attitude that is open to love and new experiences despite our imperfect past. In order to have spiritual ecstasy, we need to be free from the chains of hesitation that hold us back and allows ourselves to be bold in spirit, unafraid of "what ifs."

So, how can we strengthen our spiritual lives? There are many available paths on this journey, but on a scale of 1-10, think about how often you are willing to do each of the following:

1. Are you hopeful, looking forward to the future with confidence? Or do you see no possibility for a solution, even if it may merely be something you cannot imagine at this particular time? Say to yourself, 'I am a pessimist' and 'I am an optimist' and see how that feels inside your core. If you are a pessimist, you are a prophet of doom, which is your choice. But personally, I am not going to invite a "kill-joy" into my life, so you can hang out with all of those other cynics and live your life in misery. You are free!

2. What strategies do you employ to generate inner peace? A connection to your environment? Serenity and tranquility are developed in your spirit by practicing calm through prayer, meditation, looking at the clouds, singing with all of your soul, completely enjoying chewing and tasting whatever is in your mouth, whatever takes you there. Let your spirit move you by practicing all kinds of creative methods of leading you to experience bliss. Do you believe in an after-life? Is the concept you have about what that might look like helpful or distressing?

3. If you are religious, do you attend church, mosque, or temple? Do you leave the service feeling stronger in your faith, eager to face the world with all of its challenges? If you are Native American, have you been active with ceremonies, dance, and feast days? Is your tribe a high priority? If you are Wiccan, have you been in awe of the nature unfolding around you? Do you practice being a part of the earth, and not attempt to own it?

4. Do you pray, meditate, or use guided imagery to ease your troubled mind by soothing yourself with various mantras? Examples might include, 'Everything is okay. I am safe.' What about, 'No one can take anything away from me, I have what I need.' Or, 'I can handle hard times, I've done it before.' Finally, 'I cannot run out of love, I will always have plenty.'

5. Do you believe that having a purpose in life is important? Can you express what this means for you? Is doing your best every day sufficient, or do you practice regret and self-judgment because you are not perfect?

6. Do you communicate kindness and sincerity? Do you value healthy connections that foster a sense of safety where you can be your true self and show respect for others by acting in a loving manner? Do you demonstrate compassion when you find people who are suffering, showing concern, and offering support?

7. Are you able to calmly accept whatever may happen, or do you have a tendency to become easily alarmed and attempt to control things you do not have control over?

As I mentioned earlier, say to yourself, "This, too" as a way to accept what is difficult and certainly nothing you had planned. "This too," means life will continue to unfold for you and without your permission.

8. Are you optimistic about life, trusting that life knows how to take care of itself, and you are not in charge of everything? Do you understand that when you realize you are in charge of yourself and you have the power to change you, peace and contentment will follow? This is because you're letting go of trying to control other people, places and things.

9. Do you protect your spirit by being brave, and practice courage by saying "No" to others who are attempting to control you and don't respect you as Sheriff? Are you able and willing to recognize when you may be in the presence of a sociopath; a person who will take your money, spouse, or manipulate your spirit without feeling remorse? Have you considered how you will be remembered after you die, that your words and deeds will be your legacy? Do you realize the tremendous power you have every day to make the world a better place? The capacity to change the course of history is available to you every day. How are you changing history while you still have time?

Spiritual Strength Assessment

Look within yourself and determine if you are closer to rating your spiritual strength a number 1, 'I do not think about my spiritual power, I don't even know what that means for me.' Or a 5, 'Sometimes I am aware of promoting my inner piece, courage, and purpose I have for myself and others, but a lot of the time I don't pause to consider this.' Or perhaps you're a 10, 'I believe my journey here is important, and I can make an enormous difference in my own life and the lives of others by being spiritually strong. I am paying attention to my spirit.' You are only as spiritually strong as you are focused on growing your spiritual strength.

CHAPTER 12

Measuring Your Social Strength

Social strength is the fourth element or tip on our Power Badge. Social strength means standing up for what is right, even if you are standing alone. Social strength comes from the power of being just fine with who you are, without a need for approval from anyone else. When you interact with other people, social strength means having the confidence that no one can force you to be someone you are not. When you decide you will not be manipulated by others, there is a much smaller chance they will be able to persuade you. Having good friends also really helps. Choose your friends wisely, and reject people in your life who are insulting, try to make you doubt yourself, have negative beliefs, and other traits you do not want for yourself. Relationships and social life at work are formal and being friendly and cheerful to everyone is what professional behavior looks like. We work with some people we would not invite over for Sunday dinner, and that is just fine. Being emotionally mature socially means you decide to have people in your social world who bring you joy and laughter, the gift of encouragement, and accept you for who you are. Just because an individual is a relative does not mean you have an obligation to provide time and love, you do not.

So, how can we strengthen our social lives? Consider these strategies and conditions:

1. What are you bringing to your social relationships? Kindness, a sense of humor, words of encouragement, interesting conversations, thoughtfulness, sensitivity?

One of the most challenging opportunities and most meaningful connections with those we love occur when we or the person we care about have been hospitalized or become very ill. Visiting to merely show up because you care, is love. You can take lollipops or mints to help keep mouths dry, lip balm to keep lips wet, cream to rub on your loved one's hands and feet, a book or magazine or newspaper to read to them. Ask if you can turn off the television during your visit. It is distracting and makes communicating difficult to accomplish. When those you love need you, show up for them.

2. Do you treat the people in your social world like you want them to treat you? Do you love the way you want to be loved?

One of the chief complaints in social relationships is that the other person doesn't "get me," or "doesn't seem to listen," appears to be "distracted" or shows "no affection." If these gifts are important to you to receive, check yourself before you wreck yourself and make sure you are giving as much as you would like to receive. Most people will follow your cue and become more present with you, if this is how you are with them. If not, perhaps you need to spend more time with people who are considerate and value the fact they have another opportunity to be with you.

3. Maintaining valuable social relationships means you need to invest the time and show the other person you value him or her in your life. Do you send birthday cards, write letters, or keep in touch by telephone, text, or email? Do you buy gifts, make meals, buy people lunch or dinner, and display other behaviors that exude a generous spirit?

If you are on Facebook, simply taking the time to acknowledge a post a friend made can make someone's day. Letter writing is becoming less popular, mostly because it is "not fast enough," I have been told more than once. Expressing yourself in a letter is not only glorious for your receiver to absorb and cherish, but it is also a great exercise for you to remember what is important that has been happening in your life that you would like to describe and share. Letters are like living time capsules and I encourage you to write at least one a month, simply because I believe it will bring great joy to yourself and others.

4. Do you keep in touch with people you care about who have moved, retired or become ill?

This is especially important for the elderly people in your life who do not have texting or other social media skills. Remember the older you get the harder it is to hear, especially on the phone. One more reason to write a letter, a poem, draw a picture, something to create and put in the mailbox that will elevate mood and bring joy.

5. Are you a person you would want to hang out with? Are you satisfied with your personality, or could you become more likable with a more loving spirit?

Do you spend time with others who belong to different ethnic groups and cultures? Have you been bold enough to nurture relationships with people from other countries, others who look different from you, come from different parts of your city, state, and country? A large part of what makes you an interesting person is you invite people into your circle who can teach you about how to live life with a different mindset and who practice unfamiliar rituals. Be open-minded with different kinds of people and different pigments of color to their skin. Remember, there is no such thing as "race." That is a human construct designed in the 18th century to justify using and owning other humans of color, as slaves. Have friends who are people with different skin colors from your own. They are typically quite interesting and need to be cherished members of your species. If you are fortunate, they will have different stories to tell and lessons to share if they find *you* to be good company.

6. Are you taking the time to be social by belonging to a group or club with people who share your interests?

You don't have to be a "joiner" to have some fun belonging to a bowling team, book club, habitat for humanity group, or leader of a scout troop. You just need to celebrate the positive connections you will make with other people, rather than calling your television your best friend. Not to be judgmental, if you want to spend your social life completely with your television, go for it, Sheriff. Just remember, television is not real life, but merely a production created for a television audience.

7. Do you allow yourself to bring relationships to a close that have become toxic for whatever reason?

This is not easy, but it's necessary. Remember there are many people you will make friends with in the future. Do not stay in relationships out of fear you will become lonely. Don't settle for being in relationships with negative people. You deserve to receive what you give to others; your optimism, encouragement, love, listening skills, and the joy of being comical and often having a good laugh. If you are with someone and you think, *Wow, I would rather be alone than be with this person*, that is your cue you need to leave the relationship, or at a minimum, spend as little time as possible with this person you can tolerate, but would rather not.

8. Are you open to meeting people who are so unfamiliar to yourself you embrace this as a tremendous opportunity to understand humans in a new way?

This will challenge you to be friendly and assertive when meeting new people, especially if they look like they are not from around these parts. Let us be hopeful that different ethnicities will make their way into your life. It is exciting and can even be motivating to learn how life can be lived with perspectives developed by all kinds of Sheriffs from around the globe. They have something very different to give to you, embrace it.

9. Do you invite friends over for dinner, game night, lunch, or parties? Do you ask friends who have moved away to come for a visit for vacation or a long weekend? Are you taking the time to cultivate the relationships with the people you love and want to have in your life?

It takes work to cultivate and maintain relationships. This is something you choose to value and have in your life, or not.

Don't wait for "them" to reach out because that may not happen. You will have a wonderful social life if you consciously build and develop one, it doesn't happen by chance.

10. If you consider yourself a loner, is that by choice or out of insecurity and unwillingness to take the risk of feeling vulnerable with others at a social event?

You may or may not like the crowd, but you won't have an interesting life if your friends all live inside your television or telephone apps. You decide if you are brave enough to share life experiences with those who may in fact be the most interesting people you have ever met. Be open socially, this is an enormous strength and affords you the opportunity to grow your social power. If you feel uneasy being a part of large groups, then put yourself inside of smaller ones, and enjoy your one on one experience with relationships. We are social animals and need the opportunity to practice delivering social strength to our communities.

Social Strength Assessment

Think about how you spend your free time and with whom. Do you isolate yourself out of fear of rejection or to protect yourself because of bad relationships? We all have done this to some extent.

On our previous scale of 1-10, if you are not willing to risk any relationship for fear that it may not be a good one, or if you don't even enjoy spending time with yourself, give yourself a 1. If you think, 'I typically enjoy being with myself because usually I think I am fun, reasonable, and understanding, but sometimes I don't engage in social events or risk meeting new people because I worry I won't fit in or have a good time,' give yourself a 5. Are you the life of the party, and have to keep establishing boundaries around your time because so many people want you in their lives? On a typical day, do you crack yourself up and enjoy thinking about your life? If this is the case, you are a solid 10 and socially strong.

CHAPTER 13

Measuring Your Sexual Strength

Your sexual strength begins the moment you open your eyes in the morning until you fall asleep at night. It includes the ability to appreciate your erotic nature, to relate to yourself and your lover(s) with pleasure, feeling appreciative of your sexual appetite being satiated once again with new memories to savor. Sexual strength is a significant part of who you are and how you show yourself to the world.

Sexual strength is more than just having fun when you have sex, although this is one of life's greatest joys and satisfactions. It is imperative you remember you own your sexuality, and how you express it with yourself and a partner(s) is a basic human right. Your sexual identity is your personal concept of self as male, female, a blend of both or neither. Your gender identity can be the same or different from your sex assigned at birth. How you express your gender identity is through your behavior, haircut, voice, and clothing which may or may not conform to socially defined characteristics typically associated with being either masculine or feminine. The good news is that society has evolved and more and more people are being accepted for how they feel as a sexual being on the inside. The challenge remains when people are prejudiced and ignorant towards folks who are expressing sexuality in a nontraditional way. Do not tolerate hate and disrespect, for you are worthy and valuable exactly how you are. Your sexual strength is how positive you feel about your sexuality, and living with confidence and pride in your skin. Your sexual power grows stronger when you release any shame or regret and move forward as the sexual being you are right now.

So how can you strengthen your sexual life? Consider using these assessments for how you believe you are being sexual throughout your life:

1. Are you getting your sexy on? Do you get your sexy back after intense participation in activities where you are completely focused on tasks that exclude your sexual awareness? Do you read, watch, fantasize, or actively facilitate your erotica?

2. Are you empowered by your sexuality, knowing you can feel sexy or be sexual on your terms? Do you feel confident in saying "No" to sexual overtures and requests? Do you realize you are never obligated to have sex?

3. Are you exploring your sexual freedom by taking the lead in sexual encounters and expressing yourself verbally and nonverbally? Do you ask for what you want? Are you a giving lover?

4. If you are open to having multiple partners, separately or all at once, are you respectful to everyone in the room being on your same page, that this is acceptable to them? If you are into kink, is your partner?

5. If you enjoy flirting and/or being flirted with, are you aware of the other person being nonverbally/verbally open to playful allure? Flirting does not necessarily mean, 'I want to have sex with you.' Typically it means, 'I find you romantic or attractive so I am going to play with your emotions for a while.' If someone's flirting is making you feel uncomfortable, do not hesitate, stop. If the person you are flirting with appears to be uncomfortable (you may have misread their openness towards you), again stop immediately. Flirting with strangers can signal that you want to have casual sex with them, so flirt with caution with people you have just met. If you are married, flirting with your spouse needs to be the terrain where you practice this skill. Otherwise, you are opening a door that

is communicating that you are open to sexual possibilities outside of your marriage/committed relationship.

6. Remember the biggest sexual organ we have is between our ears. Your mind and how it has developed over the years has the biggest impact on your sexual strength. What stories have you told yourself about your sexuality? How sexy do you believe your body is? Do you believe your genitals are incredible, or disgusting? Do you believe your body is attractive and desirable, or have you created judgmental beliefs about how you look naked, how your skin feels, or how your face looks when you are having an orgasm? In other words, who have you created in your mind? Are you desirable or embarrassing? You may need to create a more loving, hot and excited mindset. Conversely, you may need to envision appreciating the other person's attractiveness instead of concentrating solely on your own.

7. While it is preferable to live life with sex appeal, remember there are those who will sexualize you in an unwelcoming manner. This may include everything from staring at your body and making you feel uncomfortable because the gaze is long and intrusive, to putting their hands on you uninvited, or attempting to touch you or have sex with you without your permission. Use your body language and voice to command the person to cease and desist. Be serious and intense so the message is, 'Back way off from me.' Monsters will try and take what belongs to you sexually and assault you. Be ready to use

any means possible and available to try to get away quickly. Some may believe they have the right to dominate and take your sexual power. Try however you can, to cause this person physical harm by inflicting grave injury so you may flee and call the police.

8. If you are unable to flee an attacker, remember that you are not alone. One in three women and one in five men have been sexually abused and/or raped. If this happens to you, seek counseling to help you take your power back and overcome symptoms from the trauma of the assault. You do not need to live your life wishing it could have been different for you. Make it different for you now, on your own terms. Do not let your attacker continue to harm you by not taking care of yourself to heal your emotional, spiritual, and social injuries.

9. You can leave sexual trauma behind by living your life with sexual purpose, by being in charge of your sexual expression. Define what you want your sexuality to look and feel like, and you can reclaim your power. Say to yourself, 'Never again. I lived through the terror and I will not let it define me. I will own my sexual power and prepare myself so that if another predator attempts to harm me, they will be the one who will have to live with the suffering inflicted by me. I am not afraid.' Sexual trauma is prevalent in our society, and some people choose not to share their experiences with others. Be respectful that this history may exist for your lover.

10. Are you taking care of your sexual health? It takes courage to get tested, get annual exams, and talk to a physician about physical symptoms manifesting in your most private body parts. It's okay, they have heard it before.

11. Sex is perfect with the perfect person. Is your lover right for you? Do they treat you with respect, love, and tenderness, or do they mistreat you? Are they having an affair? If so, is this a deal-breaker? If you are legally married, an affair is a violation of the contract. Seek counsel from others if you need to. You are not in this alone, Sheriff. Remember, you are never alone.

Sexual Strength Assessment

Think about your sexual strength and how it lands on our scale. You have earned 1 point if, 'I allow unsolicited touching and flirtations from others. I have never healed from my sexual abuse. I avoid sex.' Maybe you're closer to a 5, 'If it were a perfect world, I would be more careful and practice safe sex. I sometimes don't communicate what I need when I am in an intimate situation with another person.' Or perhaps you're a 10, 'If I want to have an orgasm and my partner is not available, I find great joy and satisfaction when I masturbate and I touch myself and my lover with respect and confidence during lovemaking.' Finally, 'I will shut down unwanted advances without care or concern for who the other person is or how they are going to respond to my assertiveness and the volume of my voice.' Sexual power is sexual confidence.

CHAPTER 14

Measuring Your Emotional Strength

How dull would life be if we did not feel our emotions? Passionate, moving, touching, sentimental, heart-warming, and dramatic emotions are what great songs and stories are based upon. This ability to feel is what makes us human. When we meet someone who seems aloof, detached and even cold-blooded, most of us will put up an emotional boundary because they seem vacant or indifferent to our presence. Knowing what is going on emotionally with oneself is a skill that takes practice, and it is worth the effort. Emotional strength means you are confident about how to identify what you are feeling so you may proceed wisely. The four major emotions we have are fear, joy, sadness and anger. To learn how to become friends with our feelings is to respect them as our trusty guides, informing us at the moment how we are reacting to thought and circumstance on an instinctual level. If you trust your gut you are already in a healthy emotional state of living your life to the fullest. No one has the privilege of feeling your feelings except you, and the goal is to enjoy and appreciate the gift of living a passionate life.

I have worked with clients who presented a wide variety of emotional problems. The following examples of people in distress reflect how folks can exist on either end of the spectrum of emotional expression.

When I met Rebecca I was impressed with her professional appearance. She had a sharp business suit on and carried herself with great confidence, taking my hand with a firm handshake and giving me direct eye contact. She introduced herself as I am sure she had done a thousand times before, with a relaxed style and friendly look on her face. Yes, she was a saleswoman.

When I asked what I could help her with during our session, she reported her fiancé informed her that if she did not start expressing her emotions with him, he wasn't sure if they could proceed with the marriage and the children they talked about raising together. 'He's a counselor, like you, so I get it.

I love him and want to get married, but I cannot turn something on that I don't have. I don't really understand him because we have really good sex, a lot. He's a guy, so does he want me to cry when I have an orgasm, or what?'

I asked her if he had given her any specific examples of what he needs or would like her to give to him, and she said, 'He describes me as an empty shell like there is something "missing." My clients adore me and I make more money than I know what to do with. I really believe this is his problem.'

It is common to do a little digging in the counseling relationship to find out what has happened in the past that has not been revealed by the client. My intuition and experience were telling me this client had some sort of trauma history and she figured out how to live with it by hiding emotional vulnerability, even with her fiancé, the person she trusted the most. One of the requirements to be an effective counselor and helping people is having the detective skills to be a trustworthy sleuth, in my humble opinion. That means asking probing questions that get to the root of the problem without spending two months trying to figure it out. So I asked her,

'Rebecca, will you please tell me about the worst day in your life?'

Her expression did not change, but she cleared her throat and said, 'It's kind of a long story, do we have time?' she asked.

'My schedule is clear for the rest of the afternoon. I have two and a half hours until we close," I responded.

'Alright then, the worst day of my life was the day I was almost murdered,' she revealed.

We used every minute of those 2.5 hours, and she told me one of the most horrific stories I have ever heard. There were a lot of details in how she met this psychopath, how he ended up in her home and the actual attack that she survived because she took yoga, ran daily, and had the balance, core, and leg strength to keep kicking him and kicking him while he was stabbing her with kitchen knives. She finally crawled through a window with him stabbing her legs as she escaped to the ground. A neighbor was taking his trash out for the next day's pickup and he saw her and ran over. She probably would not have survived without this good fortune to be spotted falling out of the window and covered in her and her attacker's blood. She fought back with all of her might and survived because she was in good physical condition and because she had a caring neighbor who did not just go back inside of his house at the sign of trouble.

'Have you told your fiancé this story, Rebecca?' I asked.

'Yeah, after we started dating and he came over to my house and saw the holes in the walls from the fight. I told him I hadn't gotten around to fixing them after a fight, and he offered, so I said yes, please. I barely knew him so I gave him the short version of the story. 'Some guy came over and tried to beat me up,' was the version of the attack, like I told my family and employer. You are the only person who really knows what happened beside the police.'

Rebecca had never received counseling for this trauma and admitted she had "kinda shut down" when talking about her emotional life. 'It just feels better to live in the now, you know what I mean?'

We came up with a treatment plan that included relationship counseling where she could have a safe space to talk to her fiancé about how she has been coping with almost losing her life.

'It's worth a shot, I think I would really miss him if we broke up.'

'He needs to know what a fierce warrior you are, Rebecca,' I told her. 'He needs the opportunity to feel gratitude he's got you in his foxhole.'

I do not know if the couple's counseling was successful, because I wasn't the provider. However, what I do know is when you turn yourself off emotionally, people who know what depth and intimacy feel like in relationships, will not feel this with you, and it won't be enough for them. I recommend you decide that denying your emotions is not enough for you, either. You have the right to live your life with the full range of emotional experience, despite your traumatic history.

Emotional strength means you are actively committed to fostering your resilience when difficulty arises. You are aware of having emotions and can describe what those are for yourself, you are able to define yourself as content, meaning you feel fulfilled and are at peace. Everyone faces ups and downs of everyday life, and emotional strength is about consciously managing the feelings that come with the complicated privilege of being a human being. Let's say you have a big job interview. It's not uncommon to feel nervous and a bit of anxiety as you prepare for a new experience. You will feel emotion when you are mistreating yourself with negative self-talk such as, 'These people are going to think I am unqualified,' as you walk into the job interview. Your brain will believe whatever you tell it, so if you set yourself up with a disrespectful message, you are going to feel anxious and you are not good enough nor worthy of the job. Your feelings come from your beliefs, so believe this when walking into that interview, 'I am a professional who enjoys people and I am ready to get to work. I am excited about being able to work here, and I will tell this to the interview team.' Thinking and speaking to yourself in this way will build your emotional strength.

On the other end of the emotional spectrum was a client named Mario, whose tears were always at the surface of his emotions. He worked with children and stated this type of job kept him happy because children were such a good "distraction." He was tearful from the beginning of our session together and kept apologizing for being "so emotional."

I told him, 'I have lots of tissues, most people cry with me. I am really comfortable with your tears.' He started crying harder and told me it had become embarrassing at family gatherings, at the movies, any time he began to feel anything emotionally it always came out as tears.

'Mario, you are a sensitive soul and that is okay. Our goal in counseling is for you to be in control of your emotions, and for your emotions to follow your instructions. Are you in?' I asked him.

'Oh yes, please help me,' he said.

I asked him to tell me the story of his narrative, what he typically says to himself throughout the day. Crying much harder now, he whispered,

'I am just a little sparrow. I fly and fly and I am still afraid. I am worthy of real love, I matter.'

'Who hurt you?' I asked him.

We began a counseling relationship with the goal to help him become in control of his emotions, even though he had been repeatedly raped as a child by a close family friend. The work of forging an adult identity with a powerful emotional voice capable of setting boundaries and truly believing he was safe, began. He was a Sheriff but did not know it at the beginning of our work together. Mario healed, grew stronger, and told me he was spreading the message, 'Go get your Power Badge from Dr. Bain!' What a ferocious Sheriff.

Your emotional strength has the ability to grow if you decide that your emotions are dear friends you like and trust. If you believe your emotional life can help you navigate and enjoy your day, then you have the desire to experience and react to emotions in a helpful and positive manner. You are responsible for making judgements about yourself and taking yourself to an emotional location that is fearful, angry, sad or joyful. It is completely up to you depending on your frame of mind and what you choose your reaction to the circumstances is going to be.

Assess your past "go-to" emotional reactions. If you tend to "freak out" this means you go to the panic mode which is fear. If you usually "lose your temper" or "get riled up" or you charge into an anger web, are you trying to control something that is out of your control? Feeling anger means something needs to change, so be aware of whether or not you need to change yourself or you need to change your circumstances. If you usually "get lonely" or feel misunderstood or rejected, you have just walked headfirst into sadness and depression.

If you usually feel joy, you are practicing self-love and compassion for yourself and others. Your narrative probably sounds something like this, "I treat myself the way I treat others, with patience, curiosity, understanding and a joyful welcoming with some love thrown in for good measure. I trust myself and believe I have a duty and obligation to treat myself as the best friend I have ever had. Therefore, I will make a promise to myself to have a happy and open heart to myself and others, knowing no one has the power to make me feel anything without my permission. If I feel myself getting 'hooked' by a manipulator, I will take a deep breath and ask myself for confidence, telling myself to stay cool, calm, and collected – the "3 Controlled Cs."

Your emotional strength is dependent on you being aware of your emotional reactions and whether or not they are constructive and helpful or just a bad habit of becoming reactive emotionally rather than experiencing how you feel in the moment, and why. I compare this to lifting weights. The more often you build your emotional awareness, the stronger you will become. You will have deeper relationships because you have the skills that help you manage your emotions and ongoing awareness. You will show more empathy and compassion because you are not stressing about how what happened is affecting you. You will be able to talk about your feelings from the adult person inside your heart, rather than the child you used to be, who has no insight into why certain emotions are coming to the surface.

Strong emotional power means higher self-esteem because you see and/or look for your brave heart, having the confidence you can deal with the good, the bad, and the ugly. Whatever happens next and yes, there are more tests and tragedies to come, you will have the confidence you can cope because you have been practicing good habits around positive self-talk. Hanging out with other people who are emotionally healthy, reading books that have tips on how to take care of yourself and your other relationships will help you build you strength. Creating an ongoing assignment for yourself, to invent new scripts when that old negative voice talks to you and creates a space in your emotions that tells you terrible tales of woe and generates negative scenarios is a step in the right direction. Remember your emotions belong to you and you must take responsibility for them, just like every other component of your Power Badge that makes you feel invincible because you are in charge, Sheriff.

Emotional power involves consciously reframing beliefs about life and creating the kind of feelings you want to live with. Own your emotions with pride, Sheriff, knowing you have the control to either be with them at the moment or can come back to them at a less vulnerable time. However, you will find yourself in emotional trouble when you exaggerate the truth of a given situation and use your subsequent reaction to justify your excessive response. This can also be described as "Having a 10-dollar reaction to a 10-cent problem." Emotions are subjective responses we have trained ourselves to feel, like love or fear. With time and practice, we can discipline ourselves when having an emotional reaction to strengthen our self-control.

Consider each of the following:

1. Are your emotions easily stirred by what other people say and do, or do you feel in control of your emotions regardless of what others are saying and doing?

2. Do you feel responsible for other people's reactions, or do you recognize that other people's behavior is their responsibility and out of your control? Remember, Sheriff, that you need to allow others to own their emotions just as you so proudly own yours.

3. There are four major emotions to concentrate on; fear, anger, sadness, and joy. Are you able to identify what emotion is causing you to feel a certain way? For example, do you practice saying to yourself, 'Okay, am I feeling fear, anger,

sadness, or joy?' Can you admit to yourself when you have gone into the subjective mode and left the world of facts, compared to what is objectively real?

4. How often do you experience fear? Fear can be a good thing. It can protect you with instincts like run, hide, or fight, from someone or something dangerous. Fear can also motivate you to positive stress to perform well at work so you keep your job. Fear helps you guard yourself emotionally, so you are not manipulated or taken advantage of. It can help you stick to a budget, so you do not lose your home or go bankrupt. However, fear can become excessive. For example, when people fear germs and wash their hands raw or will not leave the house because they are afraid of strangers. Do you have any fears that bring negative consequences into your life?

5. How many times a day, week, or month do you feel angry? Do people often annoy you? Do you become hostile when life does not go according to plan? Do you feel a strong feeling of displeasure frequently because you tend to be cynical and negative? Are you often aggressive? Anger is best utilized as a signal that something needs to change. Your brain will believe what you tell it, so are you training your brain to be angry or do you focus on more positive thoughts?

6. How often are you in a state of sadness or unhappiness? Do you feel depressed and if so, how often? When there is a loss in your life, do you allow yourself to grieve and lean

on others for support and encouragement? Everyone needs to heal from sadness. Are you giving yourself time, perhaps a lifetime, to learn how to cope so your grief eventually evolves into triumph, even if that triumph is deciding not to commit suicide?

7. If you are happy be sure and tell that to your face. Joy is almost everyone's favorite emotion. How often do you feel pleasure, contentment, love and affection for yourself and others? Do you laugh and smile easily or does there need to be a special occasion for you to enjoy life? Do you tend to not pay attention to the present, even though this is where humor and joy are typically found? Do you tell yourself life is to be enjoyed or endured? Are you positive and hopeful – or pessimistic, quick to self-doubt and put yourself down?

8. How often do you nurture yourself emotionally? Every minute? Every day? Rarely? Do you focus on creating the reality you want to live in? What type of personality are you cultivating? Is it someone others want to be with, including yourself? Do you give of yourself emotionally, feeling, and displaying a passion for life, other people, or a favorite charity or cause? Do tend to be selfish with your emotions, typically behaving in a guarded, rigid manner that exudes mistrust rather than confidence? Do you know when you need to be formal emotionally (e.g. at work, with strangers) and when you can be informal (close friends, lovers)?

9. Emotional strength means you have the capacity to show compassion and understand other people's feelings, situations or motives. Do you consider that a large part of your legacy on this planet will involve being remembered by people you have been kind to and helped along the way? Will people remember you as charming, easygoing, fun-loving, happy, giving, generous and interesting? Or will your legacy be one of being difficult to get along with, selfish, egotistical, angry, anxious, and aloof? Will people say you were quick to guard your emotions, rather than being emotionally present?

10. Do you have faith in yourself so that you feel confident? Do you let go of past emotions or do they come back and haunt you, robbing you of potential opportunity and goodwill? Are you willing to dispute emotions that are not serving you well by using your creativity to think about life in new ways, giving yourself opportunities to feel differently? You cannot hang out with negative people and immerse yourself in negativity like too much horrible news, television, books and still live a positive life. We recreate our emotional worlds by using our minds to enjoy new belief systems. Your inherent worth does not depend on your emotions or mood. Do you remember that no matter how you feel, you have an obligation to yourself to have a meaningful life? And that, "This too shall pass?"

Emotional Strength Assessment

In thinking about your emotional strength, give yourself a 1 if you feel like a scared rabbit that always runs away from the unknown, thinking of things like, 'I would take the chance, but I will probably fail and get hurt in the process.' Or maybe you are closer to a 5, 'If I could just get a break and meet more people similar to me I would be able to be more giving. I feel depressed sometimes and then I don't have the pep to find humor in things, although I want to.' Or perhaps you're an emotional giant 10, 'I take responsibility for rewiring my emotional self by believing I can and will do so throughout the course of my life, gaining confidence that my feelings can be not only changed, but nurtured and accepted for what they are. My emotions are my best friends, and I respect them for giving me passion for this life, to truly feel my existence here.'

It is positive, nurturing, loving self-talk that are the keys to unlocking the door leading to emotional confidence, bliss, strength and well-being. Practice your emotional strength scripts often and they will automatically appear in your consciousness, promoting an emotional identity you can not only live with but be proud of. Write down 10 "go-to" sentences that fit for you when you need a cheerleading squad.

Remember, let yourself feel with abandon when you are watching a great movie, attending an Opera or a concert, when you listen to the radio or your music, when you are dancing to rockin' music, when you are feeling in love, when you are enjoying a belly laugh, or when you are holding a baby. Enjoy your excitement when taking a stand or winning a prize. Enjoy your emotions, for it is those visceral feelings deep inside you that can fill you with passion and love.

Power Badge Assessment

And so, in our six-pointed badge of mental, physical, spiritual, social, sexual, and emotional strength add up your points from each section, Sheriff, and see how close to 60 points you are today. Assessing your Power Badge is an exercise that needs to be practiced at least several times a year. Checking on your progress is an important gift to give to yourself. Do not be judgmental of the number, but appreciative that you have clarity and an authentic read of your strength. You know yourself better than anyone else. Trust yourself, look at the strengths that you have with new questions along the way to determine your progress. If your number dips rather than rises, pat yourself on the back for having the courage to take an honest look at yourself. Only the strongest person has a willingness to say to herself/himself, 'I can do better.'

I believe you will grow stronger and better as you gain more knowledge and inspiration. Ride your horse into your sunset with your head held high, knowing you are brave and good. I think Me Town is a spectacular addition to everything that is, and I want you to know and believe that, too. Enjoy your ride and remember – Me Town belongs to you.

_____, **Sheriff**

Your Signature Here

Resource: The Me Town Sheriff's A-Z Guide

Before you end this book I want to leave you with a handy resource and a quick reference guide to help you in Me Town. Use this when you need a quick reminder of how to move forward in life. There is a reference word for each letter of the alphabet. Don't ever forget your words are important, Sheriff, and so are your ABC's. You have your special alphabet of keywords to help keep you on track as you run Me Town. Mount up and let's ride through. Sit tall in your saddle, Sheriff. Your life belongs to you.

A = ACCEPTANCE

What do you need to accept?

Has anyone ever said to you, 'Just accept it, life happens?' I'll bet they have. But the ability to see things as they **really** are requires courage. Acceptance is a process we must ultimately engage in even if we feel fear, anger, or sadness. It is part of our thought process when we think to ourselves, *I can do this. I am strong enough to handle it.* You don't have to enjoy, admire, or like what happens. If you get dealt a bad card, for example, the job is over or the relationship has ended, know you can play it any way you choose. Grieve the lost potential and know a new card is waiting for you in the deck. If you hold on to what is not healthy or good for you, the game of life will not go well for you, Sheriff. Remember, practice acceptance and play to win.

Value acceptance as a way of becoming a stronger person. Repeat these words, 'I will not resist what I cannot change. I will accept it and feel calm and relieved because I have to let it be. Accepting reality cannot hurt me but denying it can.'

B = BELIEFS

When we believe something it means we are confident that it is true. Our beliefs shape our thinking and how we approach everything in our lives. What we sometimes forget is that our belief systems are based on ingrained habits and patterns of thinking, rather than us choosing to look at life in a new way. If you are suffering it is likely because of how your beliefs impact your feelings about yourself or your life. If you want to thrive and be joyful consider new beliefs that will take you there.

Take an inventory and write down ten things you believe about yourself,

Ten things you believe about other people, and

Ten things you believe about the rest of the world.

Next to each belief, write how that belief makes you feel, affects your outlook, and alters your perspectives. If some of these beliefs are negative, write down how you can make them positive instead. For example, if one of your ingrained beliefs is that you don't have much to offer others, focus on changing that. Start making a list of your good qualities. Are you chivalrous? Do you smile at others? Do you feed a stray cat in your neighborhood? Read these qualities often and keep reading them until you recognize that your kindnesses make a difference, and you will eventually start to believe it.

A positive mindset and beliefs will help you avoid unnecessary worry and live a more fulfilling life. You have the power to open your mind and explore new, healthier beliefs, Sheriff.

C = CATALYST

A catalyst is something that brings about a change. You are the force that ignites change for yourself. Valuing a fresh approach helps you think objectively and avoid automatic reactions to life. This enables you to make good decisions that can take you in new, exciting directions.

Your catch rope hangs from your saddle and it is one of the best tools you own. Toss that rope over your head and throw hard with your arm and shoulder, using all of your strength.

If you miss the target, begin again and ignite your passion to boldly conquer what you desire. Do not give up, for you are the catalyst that makes your dreams come true. You can also be the spark that spurs others to make changes and alter the course of their destiny.

D = DANGER

Danger is always present in Me Town. Make friends with danger and you will not be as afraid. Every day all of us are exposed to potential harm, risk and peril. Recognize that danger is part of life, but do not live in fear. Instead, live like a cat or your favorite mammal, with your ears up and whiskers out. Trust yourself, your instincts and reflexes. Have a creepy feeling in your gut when someone is approaching you? Trust that feeling and take action to protect yourself, whether that is to run or avoid them, call out for help or confront them. Feel like someone in your workplace is trying to undermine you? Do what you need to do to back up your work, document your efforts, and speak up for yourself.

It is your responsibility to protect Me Town from danger as best you can, Sheriff. Whether the danger is physical or emotional, from a stranger or someone you know, be ready to throw any harmful person out of Me Town. If they make you feel threatened, they don't deserve to be there. Trust your gut, and establish clear, solid boundaries with others. You are your fiercest protector. Remember, you always have your badge on. You are always in charge.

E = EXCELLENCE

What does excellence look like to you? What does "being the best" mean to you? What are your goals, and how can you be proud of yourself as you strive for them? In your everyday thoughts, words, and actions, are you conducting yourself with excellence?

This is not a practice range, Sheriff. Take your best shot every day. Try your best to hit your desired target. You will miss the bullseye sometimes, but everyone does. All of us must re-aim and keep trying. If you do this, then Me Town will be an excellent place.

F = FREEDOM

You are free to liberate yourself and become the person you want to be. Even if you are in jail or prison, you have freedom of thought and can practice independence from the oppressive thoughts you create for yourself. Right now, there are millions of people in various forms of slavery. Some human beings are unable to live their lives without oppression and violence. They are held captive. If you forget how important it is to live with the freedom of choice you have each moment, remember them. They would give anything to be you. Practice your freedom and know your rights, beginning with your right to enjoy life. Celebrate your freedom.

G = GRATITUDE

Just like the bridle that fits over the head of your horse, gratitude will guide and restrain you during your daily life choices. Lift your head up with sincere gratitude for everything you have, and everything you share with your loved ones, friends and community. Let that gratefulness lead you to make good decisions. When gratitude restrains you, it keeps you from feeling sorry for yourself. Don't dwell on negative things. Don't be resentful because you think you deserve more than other people. Be appreciative of every opportunity you have to become stronger, wiser and more authentically you.

The moment we are born, (ready, set, go!) a stopwatch begins ticking. Some people's journey to the finish line lasts only a few seconds, hours or days. You can be grateful your watch is still ticking, you still have time to think, speak and act differently. You have the time to change yourself and consequently the world. You matter. You are still here. There are millions of parts to your life you have not even discovered yet. Practice gratitude because it makes sense and feels good.

H = HAPPINESS

Happiness comes when you honor yourself. Your distinction is how you wear and take care of your hat, Sheriff. You always have your hat on, to protect your head and integrity without obligation to anyone other than yourself. Try to act in ways that align with your values, that you can be proud of. Respect yourself, and you will enjoy yourself and feel happy.

I = INTEGRITY

Your integrity is characterized by how much and how often you stick to the laws of Me Town. Your adherence to your values is what solidifies your integrity in this unpredictable world of ours. When you think and feel with integrity, you will feel complete.

J = JUSTICE

Things are not always fair in life, work, relationships, health, your genes or even the weather. You have no control over the things that are unjust in this world. The good news is you have complete jurisdiction over your own conduct, attitude, and how you treat other people. You will be betrayed by others, but you can make a commitment to yourself that you will not betray others. You will not breach or reveal confidences. You will be unwilling to lead anyone astray, but encourage them to follow their own purpose. By being fair and reasonable toward others you can create your own justice.

K = KNOW

Know that if you lay down with pigs you will get dirty. If you live, work, or socialize with negative, wily, selfish, manipulative, unhealthy people, you will either become like-minded because of their influence, or you will be chewed up and spit out by them, a shadow of your former self. Granted, sometimes we are forced into the presence of people who wouldn't hesitate to harm us (e.g., that vindictive coworker or neighbor). When there is no physical escape, know you are still in charge and can leave the room, walk inside your house, or in serious situations, report this person to management or the police. These are people who cannot be trusted. Limit your exposure and know that "you can't expect more than a grunt from a hog." These are people who do not change.

L = LIFE

A young man from a large city was visiting his elderly grandmother who lived in the country. One afternoon she said to him, 'Honey, why don't you go to the rodeo this afternoon while I make dinner for us. I bet you have never seen a rodeo before, have you?'

He replied, 'That would be a blast! Thanks, Grandma.' He took off to the county fairgrounds and found a good seat in the stands right next to an old cowboy with an enormous black ten-gallon hat.

The bull riding began, and the contestant was being thrown all over the back of a monster bull. The young man could not believe his eyes and thought the cowboy on the back might even be trampled or killed. 'I would be really upset if I had gotten that mean bull!' he whispered to the older cowboy sitting next to him. The gentleman slowly turned his head, stared right into the wide-eyed city boy, and said,

'Son, you've never been to a rodeo before, have you?'

'No sir!' the young man replied.

'Well,' the cowboy hesitated as he put some chew between his cheek and gum, 'When you ride, you want the meanest, toughest, angriest bull you can get. That way you can prove your courage, stamina and strength. It's kind of like life. Give me some difficult rides and I will show you what I am made of. Hold on during the roughest ride and you will know you have really lived.'

In that instant, the young man realized he would now welcome tough times in life. Rather than say to himself, 'Why me?' he would say, 'Bring it on. Test me. Show me what you've got.' He resolved to use all of his strength to hold on and have the best ride, no matter what.

That young man became Sheriff of Me Town that day.

M = MESSAGE

What is the message you want to send while you are on this earth? What is significant about the words you speak to yourself and to others? What is your basic theme? How do you want to be remembered? If you could put a message in a bottle and throw it into the ocean for someone to find, what would it say? If you want to bury a time capsule in your backyard, go for it. What is your message for whoever may find it? Your message is your communication with the world, what lessons you have learned and want to share, what you like to encourage people to celebrate, and what wisdom you have cultivated you want to share. Your message can be, "Please have a sense of humor" and then remember to be hilarious yourself. Your message can be, "Love is the most important gift on the planet. What about fight for the weak, they need our help?" Think about what is your daily message and if you do not have one, go ahead and create a simple truth to share. Your message is a part of the legacy you will leave behind when it is time for you to go.

N = NEW

There are always new opportunities to reinvent yourself. Stay in the present and leave the ghosts of the past behind you, for they only live in your imagination. Besides, the present time is what is new. It's easy to rely on old habits and patterns of thinking because they take little to no effort. Commit to being, thinking and experiencing what is new, and your life will be strikingly different. This is how we change. New is what makes life exciting. Trust new, do not fear it.

O = OWNERSHIP

When you take ownership of your life and who you are as an individual, you give yourself the recognition you deserve: "You are one of a kind." Claiming ownership of your life also provides self-esteem when hard times and crises come your way. Ownership as a conscious value lets you live with an identity that says, 'I own my life even though this terrible event or process is happening/has happened. It belongs to me. No one and nothing can take who I am. My life is mine.' This reality provides you with the clarity to understand your own strength, and remember everyone else is responsible for themselves. Remember who owns Me Town. You do, Sheriff.

P = POWER

You have all of the power in Me Town, all of the time. Stand on the ground like you own it. Use your body to communicate your power. Stand up tall and stick your chest out. You are the force that drives the direction you take every time you make a choice. Feel your power when you take a breath and feel it again when you let your breath go.

Your power is your degree of strength, physically, emotionally, mentally and spiritually. Like the stirrups on your horse, it supports you when you make a decision and carries you through while you take action. Your power is enormous and will help you perform at your best at home, work, and play. Practice and use your power to live your values and strengthen your identity. Your power is how bright you shine during your life. Shine so brightly that others will respect your confidence. Be reliant on yourself, the one person you know will be there for you no matter what. Love your power.

Q = QUALITY

The quality of your life depends on the quality of your perceptions. Attitude, insight, intuition, and whether you perceive your experiences positively or negatively all factor into your quality of life. Having a high quality of life takes effort. A meaningful existence does not unfold all by itself. Develop a powerful appetite for living like the passion you have for a lover and you will feel more joyful. The more you practice this, the easier it gets. Do not be fooled into believing it is your circumstances that determine the quality of your life; it is you.

R = REPUTATION

How do people feel when they hear your name? What do others think about your character? What traits and attributes would someone use to describe you? How good is your name in your social circle, family, workplace, neighborhood or community?

Your reputation is your legacy, Sheriff, both while you are alive and long after you are gone. It is a reflection of how you have lived your life in other people's eyes. What a gift you could give to the world if others said, 'I want to be like him' or 'Someday I hope to be the kind of person h/she was.'

S = SPIRIT

Your spirit is your inner being, your motivating force. It is what creates your presence in the world and how people feel when they are near you. Valuing your true meaning guides your intentions and summons that gutsy part of you that says, 'This is who I am.'

Your spirit is your essential nature. It sparks courage and determination when your sense of hope has faded. When you say to yourself, 'I am going to trust this process called chance that I have no control over,' that is your spirit speaking. Let your spirit guide you when you are not sure what to do, and your conscience will speak to you and tell you which way to go. Trust your spirit.

T = TENACIOUS

Tenacity is an admirable trait that you want to put into action as much as possible. When you are tenacious you are strong, unshakable, persistent, and unwavering. You will be able to call upon your strength of purpose, endurance, and stamina when tenacity is part of your self-identity. Life can be brutal for all of us. The goal is to survive and become stronger, knowing you have faced difficulty before and you can do it again.

Be tenacious, Sheriff.

U = UNBURDEN

The only person who can free you from an unbearable burden is you. If you are feeling oppressed by a problem, put it down. How do you cast off a burden and relieve your mind, body and spirit from fears and concerns? You can talk about it with someone you really trust, I call this emotional vomiting. You can write about it and then burn or tear apart what you have written so it is gone. Why not draw a picture of it and notice how small it really is. Breathe deeply and let your breath bring you back to this moment. There is nothing you cannot handle at this moment. Nothing. Go ahead and look at the bigger picture of your life as a whole and change your outlook. Exercise and allow your muscles and body to get the monster you have been creating out of your head. Prepare yourself a good meal and light some candles, savor every bite. Listen to your favorite music…sing along. Think about your mission statement and purpose, keep your eyes on the prize. See a counselor or rabbi or priest or minister or another spiritual guide.

There is absolutely no reason to torture or punish yourself by ruminating and swirling your thoughts in your mind. It is not real. The only real is right here and now. Feel your power and unburden yourself, Sheriff.

V = VALOR

When you value living your life as a courageous person, you are able to face danger and hardship with more confidence. You now own valor as part of your identity. To be brave you need to say to yourself, 'I can do this,' and then take the action necessary to carry out what needs to be done with true grit. Having firm determination means you won't back down from the challenge, facing it one moment at a time. That is who you are, a person with valor. Well done, Sheriff.

W = WILL

When you deliberately choose and decide on a course of action, you are exercising your free will. When you tell yourself you are free to arrive at your own decision and then act on it, you are reminded once again you have all the power to create your life. Imagine that you are the director of a movie and are responsible for telling the star of the film, YOU, how to act in every scene. Your will is in your control and you are free to act on it every second. Don't hold back, Sheriff.

X = XANADU

Every Sheriff needs a little vacation from Me Town. That is when a trip to Xanadu is in order. Xanadu is the place in your mind where you feel complete, relaxed, and blissful. Even if you can't take a vacation in real life, you can always visit your version of paradise in your imagination. Take time to seek this serenity often. Sit or lie down quietly. Envision your "happy place" – what it looks like, where it is, how it smells and tastes, who you want to invite to join you there, the time of day and night, how your body feels, how you breathe while you're there, how you smile there, the temperature and air on your skin. Be as detailed as possible. Know that when things get stressful in Me Town, you have your ticket to Xanadu in your pocket at all times.

Y = YOU

You are the only person being addressed by that negative voice in your head. When clarity is needed, old, unhealthy habits and patterns of thinking kick in, and agitation begins to brew, say to yourself, 'Hey, you!' to get your attention. It will bring you back to the present so that you can focus in peace, silencing your brain chatter. Talk to yourself with a commanding voice to help you pay attention, reframe reality, and give support, comfort, and understanding to that most prized possession of yours... After all, you are Sheriff of Me Town.

Z = ZERO

Have zero tolerance for any type of violence directed toward you, physical or emotional. If you allow anyone to be cruel, brutal, or threatening towards you, you are risking your psychological well-being and possibly your life. It is never acceptable for someone to treat you with physical, emotional or verbal violence. Do your best to stand up to a bully, whether it is your spouse, neighbor, or supervisor.

Your safety is the number one priority. Get out of harm's way immediately if you believe the danger will escalate or you cannot escape. Call the police, security, your family, or friends. You are not alone. There are people who want to help and protect you. There are resources to get you to safety.

In any crisis, if you are in immediate danger, call 911 for the police. If you cannot call 911, go to the nearest hospital emergency room to ask for help. If you cannot locate the ER, go to the nearest fire station or nearest police station where the staff will connect you with whatever crisis intervention you need.

Call National Suicide Hotline (1-800-273-8255) or Hope line Network (1-800-784-2433) if you or someone else is thinking about self-harm.

National Domestic Violence Hotline (1-800-799-7233)

National Sexual Assault Hotline (1-800-656-4673)

National Youth Crisis Hotline (1-800-448-4663)

Be reassured to know that every city and county in the U.S. has crisis intervention hotlines and assistance in place. The most important first step when you are in danger is to ask for help.

Support others who turn to you for help or if you witness them being the victims of cruelty. Have zero tolerance for violence in your life. Period.

Final Thoughts

You have come a long way, Sheriff. Do you remember the beginning of this book? Me Town was a lawless, dusty place. It was filled with rebellion, fighting, crime and fear. Then you stepped up and decided enough was enough. You took decisive action to get everyone's attention and stop the chaos. In that instant, Me Town began to change.

Now, with the help of this book, you've expanded your mind. You've broadened your perspective, thinking of yourself, your life, and situations in new ways. You've realized just how much your thoughts determine every bit of your reality and what goes on in Me Town. Changing your thoughts, beliefs and attitudes is what brings law and order to Me Town. It is now a safe place – free of the fear caused by crime, restlessness, and violence. Me Town is thriving, full of happiness, prosperity, cleanliness and peace.

You know it will take work to keep improving Me Town, and that doing so will be an ongoing process. That is okay by you. You are the Sheriff, and it's a job you love and take pride in. Me Town is your town. You have all the power. You are finally home

EPILOGUE

Today

For there is no tomorrow
And forgotten yesterday,
None to loan, nor none to borrow,
Only bold today.
There is no fancy dreaming,
Nor remembrances bitter-sweet,
No day-dreams, busy scheming,
No fortunes great to meet.
No past to ask forgiving,
No future hope to plan,
Only today in the living,
A 24-hour span.
No treasures made for keeping,
No looking up the way,
Nor tomorrow's shadows heaping,
Just living for today.

Written by my father,
Jack Arthur Bain
1925 - 1991

ACKNOWLEDGMENTS

So many thanks to all of my clients, colleagues, friends, neighbors, family, and mentors, to people in the world I have only met once and those whom I have yet to meet. You are all my teachers and trainers, and I am a curious and grateful student.

About the Author

Dr. Julia Bain, LPCC, NCC, CEAP

Since her childhood, Dr. Julia Bain has pledged to herself, her clients, friends, family and neighbors to always be proud of who you are, no matter how many times you may fall down. Teaching others to stand up for themselves, has been her focus during her 35-year career as a licensed professional clinical counselor, national certified counselor, and certified employee assistance professional. While working with people in group homes battling addiction and homelessness, providing comfort to psychiatric patients in a locked ward, giving meaning to life for those who are profoundly developmentally delayed, deaf and blind, severe mental illness, and City of Albuquerque employees and their families, she has been honored to watch the growth that results from the struggle, whatever that may be. Whether singing on her guitar in group therapy or merely bursting into song during training, Dr. Bain has always used music as a way to connect with others and promote healing.

As a 26-year career veteran in broadcasting her own television program, "Mind, Body, Spirit" on the City of Albuquerque Government Channel, she has interviewed over 100 professionals in the community including Mayor Richard Berry, informing most of her guests not to be surprised if she began to sing a few relevant lines during the interview. Julia was interviewed by the district attorney on KKOB radio as a featured guest discussing a variety of issues impacting relationships. Considered an expert in workplace violence and its impact on employees, she was interviewed by Mary Baca, LA Talk Radio, an expert working with PTSD and first responders.

As a result of her doctoral dissertation, Collection and Analysis of Baseline Epidemiological Data Among City of Albuquerque Workforce, 1997, she subsequently went on to write the City of Albuquerque's Violence Prevention and Domestic Violence Policies. Dr. Bain has been published and quoted in a variety of periodicals, including the May 2015 issue of The Employee Assistance Report, in the article she titled, "Not Here! Employees Need Help to Confront Bullies." She was also published in American Psychiatric Association Foundation July 18, 2016, Newsletter, "How to Be an Effective Supervisor – Use Your EAP." An exuberant presenter and motivational speaker, Dr. Bain has presented at the EAPA World conference, NM statewide Ombudsman Volunteer Training, Mesilla Valley Hospital and countless other venues and events. Dr. Bain's professional achievements include president of the local EAPA chapter in NM, sitting on a variety of committees and boards for agencies serving domestic violence survivors, as well as agencies serving those with addiction.

Currently, Dr. Bain is the co-owner of Me Town Enterprises, LLC, serving as a Mi Via Consultant for the Developmental Disabilities Self-Directed Waiver Program, Community Supports Coordinator for the Supports Waiver, and Support

Broker for the NM Medicaid Self-Directed Community Benefit Program for Blue Cross and Blue Shield of New Mexico and Western Sky Members for the great state of New Mexico.

Dr. Bain is a professional trainer, keynote speaker, and consults with organizations on a variety of topics, always emphasizing empowerment and the importance of self-regulation and responsibility one has to self, others and community to enjoy life, work hard, and facilitate good will and humor. Dr. Julia Bain resides in Santa Fe with her family, and loves being the best Sheriff during each moment, enjoying her YouTube channel, and celebrates her commitment to be the most loving spouse on the planet.

Mayor Timothy M. Keller presents the Executive Order proclaiming November 18, 2019, as "Dr. Julia Bain Day."

Executive Order
From the
Office of the Mayor

Whereas, Dr. Julia Bain started with the City of Albuquerque on November 12, 1991 as a counselor and was later promoted as the Employee Assistance Program Manager where she served the rest of her career over eight administrations; and

Whereas, Dr. Bain has served the City of Albuquerque for 28 years by helping to improve the mental health and overall well-being for employees; and

Whereas, Dr. Bain has tirelessly given her expertise and knowledge through training and education on a wide variety of subjects including Stress Management, Violence in the Work Place, Team Building, and Sexual Harassment; and

Whereas, Dr. Bain has provided a safe haven to those in need and to those seeking counseling during times of grief or extreme hardship; and

Whereas, Dr. Julia Bain has always presented a positive and enthusiastic attitude to those she serves and encounters each day; and

Now, Therefore, I, Timothy M. Keller, Mayor of the City of Albuquerque, do hereby proclaim, November 18, 2019, as:

"Dr. Julia Bain Day"

_____
Timothy M. Keller, Mayor

Attest:

_____
Katy Duhigg, City Clerk

19-107
Order No.

*To reach Dr. Julia for book signings, speaking engagements
and workshop facilitation:
Contact Julia@MeTown.com and
visit www.MeTown.com for assistance*

CPSIA information can be obtained
at www.ICGtesting.com
Printed in the USA
LVHW081741220421
685248LV00011B/1455